BRINGING THE JOBS HOME

ALSO BY TODD G. BUCHHOLZ

Market Shock: 9 Economic and Social Upheavals That Will Shake Your Financial Future—and What to Do About Them

New Ideas from Dead Economists: An Introduction to Modern Economic Thought

From Here to Economy: A Shortcut to Economic Literacy

BRINGING THE JOBS HOME

How the Left Created
the Outsourcing Crisis—
and How We Can Fix It

Todd G. Buchholz

SENTINEL

SENTINEL

Published by the Penguin Group

Penguin Group (USA) Inc., 375 Hudson Street, New York, New York 10014, U.S.A.
Penguin Group (Canada), 10 Alcorn Avenue, Toronto, Ontario, Canada M4V 3B2
(a division of Pearson Penguin Canada Inc.)
Penguin Books Ltd, 80 Strand, London WC2R 0RL, England
Penguin Ireland, 25 St. Stephen's Green, Dublin 2, Ireland
(a division of Penguin Books Ltd)
Penguin Books Australia Ltd, 250 Camberwell Road, Camberwell, Victoria 3124,
Australia (a division of Pearson Australia Group Pty Ltd)
Penguin Books India Pvt Ltd, 11 Community Centre, Panchsheel Park,
New Delhi – 110 017, India
Penguin Group (NZ), Cnr Airborne and Rosedale Roads, Albany, Auckland,
New Zealand (a division of Pearson New Zealand Ltd)
Penguin Books (South Africa) (Pty) Ltd, 24 Sturdee Avenue, Rosebank,
Johannesburg 2196, South Africa

Penguin Books Ltd, Registered Offices: 80 Strand, London WC2R 0RL, England

First published in 2004 by Sentinel, a member of Penguin Group (USA) Inc.

10 9 8 7 6 5 4 3 2 1

Copyright © Todd G. Buchholz, 2004
All rights reserved

CIP available
ISBN 1-59523-005-X

This book is printed on acid-free paper. ∞

Printed in the United States of America

For my father,
patriot and family man,
who heard
the whistle of a train,
the foghorn of a ship
and dreamed of where we would go . . .

Preface

Another day, another headline, another job on its way to Bombay or Beijing. America has created a jobs machine for foreigners, turning India's economy upside down (a good thing) and turning financial journalists into bashers of big business. Respected forecasters calculate that up to fourteen million Americans should be biting their nails worrying that a pink slip is waiting for them on their office chair. And for the first time, it may be America's best and brightest who face the dimmest prospects—the software writers, the legal professionals and those who got As in college mathematics.

This book navigates between two wrong-headed visions: the left-wing view that CEOs should be slapped around and borders should be slammed shut until we can assure that no one ever gets fired; and the fatalistic view that we are powerless to do anything at all but watch the market grind away.

Naturally, left-wingers and Pat Buchanan traditionalists feel comfortable slamming "greedy" executives and asserting that CEOs with bigger hearts would never send a job offshore. Baloney. CEOs are trying to build profits, serve shareholders and cut costs. American consumers benefit when they do this. Competition boosts our standard of living and allows us, for example, to buy a superpowerful computer at a laughably low price compared with ten years ago. A teenage babysitter can grab the hottest purse off a shelf at Target for less than she earns in an evening.

But the nihilistic, fatalistic ideology of many economists fails as well. *This book argues that U.S. policies on education, taxation, litigation, immigration and regulation undermine our competitiveness and push jobs away from our shores.* I estimate that they cost Americans more than sixteen million jobs and two trillion dollars of income. I believe strongly in free trade; but free trade does not mean that you ignore our domestic landscape. In the first six chapters I will examine the forces that destroy jobs at home and create them abroad. In addition, Chapter 7 explains how Hollywood's tin ear for foreign cultures costs us export opportunities. In each chapter I propose solutions, some of them quite controversial but all aimed at creating more opportunities and more prosperity.

Over the past few years, I've looked at the American job market from several perspectives: as a hedge fund manager betting on winners in the market, and as an economist and a lecturer and television commentator helping audiences navigate through a perfect storm of politics and finance. The title *Bringing the Jobs Home* does not mean that the global job market is a zero-sum game; that is, if Russia wins, we must lose. Far from it. But we can create more jobs for the U.S. economy if we liberate American workers from the foolish bureaucratic shackles that control our schools, courtrooms, immigration services and entrepreneurial sectors. My days as a White House adviser taught me that

those shackles dig deeper and feel more permanent as each sea-
son passes. Yet there is hope.

I wrote much of this book while gazing out at the Pacific, the
sun reflecting off whitecaps and rolling surf. I tell my children
that if you hop on a boat and sail toward the sunset, you will
eventually pass Hawaii en route to Japan and China. A few nifty
turns to the south will take you to India. (Experienced cruisers,
my kids ask whether the ship will offer a midnight buffet and a
Broadway show.) You would sail past more than two billion
people trying to feed their families and scratch out a decent living. Are they trying to undermine ours? No. Think of Jimmy
Stewart's 1946 movie, *It's a Wonderful Life.* In an emotional
scene, Stewart faces the evil Potter, who believes he can profit
only if he crushes others: "Just remember this, Mr. Potter: that
this rabble you're talking about, they do most of the working and
paying and living and dying in this community. Well, is it too
much to have them work and pay and live and die in a couple of
decent rooms and a bath?" If the rabble of Asia, Africa and Latin
America climb out of poverty, will we stumble backward? Non-
sense. In fact, their hopes rest on our success and the sparks of
energy and creativity that fly whenever Americans tackle a task.

If we can slip the shackles described in the chapters ahead,
we will not be crying havoc but instead celebrating freedom.

Acknowledgments

When my publisher asked me to write a book on outsourcing, I immediately jumped onto the Internet to see whether I could pay a guy in Calcutta to do it. Too many choices popped up on the screen, so I did it myself. Well, not entirely. My loving wife, Debby, and daughters Victoria, Katherine and Alexia brought me coffee, baked me cookies and snuck other treats under the door to my office as if I was a prisoner locked in a rubber room for solitary confinement. Victoria's love of the American presidents inspired me as she regaled me with stories of her favorites, especially John Adams and Ronald Reagan. Katherine and Alexia focused instead on Cinderella and Snow White, inviting me to be their prince, which these days seems like a much better job than president. And cheerful Debby kept my mind fresh by inviting me to opening nights at the La Jolla Playhouse.

I am grateful to my agent, Susan Ginsburg, and editor, Bernadette Malone, for guiding this opportunity to me. The chapter on litigation benefited from my research sponsored by the U.S. Chamber of Commerce Institute on Legal Reform and the insights of Bob Hahn, director of the AEI-Brookings Joint

Center on regulatory studies. I also thank Sam Popkin of the University of California, San Diego, for rousing my thoughts on cultural exports, Thomas Murray for advising me on the mechanics of the outsourcing business and Maria Castro for educating me on Spanish-language soap operas, though I still cannot say that I am a fan.

Thanks also to friends and colleagues like Tim Adams, Jim Carter and David Rubashkin for helping me refine my thoughts on some of the topics discussed, and my mother for celebrating my completion of this task with a tasty lobster dinner.

Contents

BRINGING THE JOBS HOME

ONE

What Are We Facing?

My father was fired. He was technologically unem-
ployed. He worked for the same firm for 12 years.
They fired him and replaced him with a tiny gadget
that does everything he does. Only it does it much bet-
ter. The depressing thing is my mother went out and
bought one.

—Woody Allen, 1968

If they fired his father today and replaced him with an Indian,
would his mother go out and get herself a svelte Sikh in a turban?
We've long gotten used to machines' pushing aside people. But
how about people's pushing aside people?

When white collars start itching, that's when we worry. Are
you sure your job is safe? A few years ago, it was just loopy Ross
Perot warning us about the giant sucking sound that would send
blue-collar jobs to Mexico. Sure enough, some Maytag riveters
in Illinois lost their jobs to a Mexican town called Reynosa. But
now IBM announces that it will hire thousands of software writ-

ers in Bangalore, India. So long to hundred-thousand-dollar jobs in Rochester and Elmira? Radiologists all over America are panic stricken that their two-hundred-thousand-dollar salaries will be shipped to India. The MRI machines may scan prone patients in American hospitals, but with high-bandwidth telecom lines, highly educated Indians can read the charts just as well as American doctors. At one-tenth the cost. The United States supplies the sick patients; Asia supplies the smart doctors and gets the money.

What happened to the euphoria for globalization, those carefree days of the late-1990s when the NASDAQ quintupled and everyone's favorite museum seemed to be the Guggenheim in Bilbao, a Spanish branch of a New York museum, designed by an LA architect? Sure, we could expect the Greenpeaceniks to protest in front of Starbucks. But why have American politicians lost their nerve and confidence in free trade? John Kerry denounced American business executives who moved business offshore as "Benedict Arnolds," as if they should wear a scarlet letter and atone. In a *New York Times* op-ed piece, New York Democrat Senator Charles Schumer actually teamed up with a former Reagan economic adviser to speak out against free trade. General Electric lost friends in Congress when it announced its "70/70/70" plan. It publicly pledged to outsource 70 percent of its head count, to push 70 percent of its outsourcing offshore and to locate 70 percent of such workers in India. Of course, GE made many new friends in New Delhi. When President Bush's chief economic adviser Greg Mankiw explained that outsourcing is just "a new way to do international trade," Democrats and Republicans demanded that Bush fire him (though they did not suggest hiring an Indian economist to take his place). Politicians began to sweat when they opened up a University of California,

Berkeley, study showing that 11 percent of U.S. jobs may move offshore in coming years. That's almost fourteen million people at risk!

What in the world is going on? Should the United States just close our doors, turn off the lights and paint GOING OUT OF BUSINESS SALE on our windows? Or should we close our borders and turn away foreign goods and talent? A few years ago, ABC News asked me to visit a Best Buy store, followed by a camera crew. I flipped over radios, TVs and DVD players like a bad juggler. I was looking for the stamps and labels that say "Made in . . ." My arms got tired before I could find a "Made in U.S.A." stamp. "China" showed up under nearly everything, with an occasional Japan, Malaysia or Taiwan. I spoke to some shoppers at the store. Did anyone hesitate to buy from Asian factories, thinking that American factories produced higher quality stuff? No. Most people thought that any radio or TV made in America might be less dependable. How ironic! Back in the 1960s a town in Japan actually changed its name to Usa so that it could stamp its exports "Made in USA" and ride on our reputation for excellence.

We have gotten used to driving Toyotas, cooking popcorn in Samsung microwave ovens and hauling massive plasma televisions that come with warranty cards written in Korean. So what's the big deal about outsourcing? While we have gotten used to American firms' hiring Mexicans and Chinese to screw or stitch together computers, refrigerators and sandals, now American firms are sending white-collar service jobs across the seas. We long gave up on Rosie the Riveter. But now Indians, Chinese and Filipinos are taking the job of Rosie the Radiologist and Raymond the Tax Accountant. These are the people who stayed in school, studied for their SATs and volunteered to flip flapjacks for their church fund-raiser. And they are worried about paying for their health insurance. When they call the insurance company to ask about a drug prescription co-pay, who answers the telephone? Come with me to a space-age campus a few miles outside of New Delhi where twenty-five hundred college-educated Indians are arriving by corporate buses. At a company called Wipro, they sit ready to pick up the phone and guide Americans through the American health-care system, most likely in a light Hindi accent. In Manila, Filipinos working for e-Telecare, one of the most successful outsourcing firms, are studying for the Series 7 exam. What is that? Ask your stockbroker, because those Filipinos are eager to buy and sell your shares, with a more courteous and pleasant tone than the manic broker with the gruff and surly voice. More than 80 percent of the Filipino agents pass the rigorous exam, compared with 59 percent for the U.S. test takers.[1]

Don't picture sweatshops and child laborers posing with Sally Struthers on a UNICEF poster. The young people answering your calls, filing your papers and diagnosing your computer bugs are sitting in front of gleaming work stations. During their breaks, they play putt-putt golf, gossip at a food court and shoot hoops pretending to be Shaquille O'Neal, or more likely, Yao Ming.

Left-Right Confusion

In 1949 Americans asked, Who lost China? Now the question is, Who lost *our jobs* to China? Unions and politicians on the left blame greedy CEOs, free trade, George Bush (both of them) and Ronald Reagan. I recently debated a French diplomat about trade who blamed General MacArthur (don't ask). Anti-free trade conservatives like Patrick Buchanan echo these arguments. Together they have inspired state legislators and governors to scream, stamp their feet and unfurl bills to halt offshore outsourcing. Arizona Governor Janet Napolitano decreed that state work must be done in the United States. Michigan Governor Jennifer Granholm ordered the state procurement office to discriminate against non-U.S. firms. Ironically, Granholm herself was not born in the U.S.A., but instead was "made in Canada."

But too many mainstream conservatives have ignored the outsourcing wave. Like Voltaire's Maître Pangloss, or more recently Bobby McFerrin, they sing "Don't worry, be happy!" They assure Americans that in the long run outsourcing makes us more efficient, cuts costs and may ultimately create more jobs at home. Why is this answer so unsatisfying—even if it someday proves true? They, too, make a crucial mistake as their knees jerk to adhere to ideology. Please follow me to their error: economists rightfully believe in free trade and conclude that if Indians can handle telephone calls more smoothly and if Chinese can screw together DVD players more sturdily, then we should not stop those Chinese DVD players from rolling off the trucks at Best Buy or hang up on the telemarketers from Bangalore.

However, free market types err when they close the door on the discussion, as if the audience should stand up and applaud the inescapable logic. I ask this question: How do businesses figure out what they should specialize in? In this book I argue that foolish government policies distort the economy and push jobs away from our shores. Of course, outsourcing reflects an efficient way of doing business—given the situation confronting firms. Of course, we should expect CEOs to strive for efficiency and cut costs, which ultimately gives American consumers more buying power. But those businessmen are often acting as they do and often finding outsourcing more efficient than hiring Americans precisely because our tax, litigation, immigration, regulation and education regimes push them out the door. It is ridiculous for liberals to blame CEOs. But let's face it: it's naïve for conservatives to blithely bless outsourcing without asking whether it may be a symptom of policy stupidity. I calculate that the policy stupidity outlined in this book costs the U.S. economy dearly.

Forget about labeling CEOs Benedict Arnolds; we should label our congressmen Douglas Corrigans. Who? Douglas Corrigan was a fan of Charles Lindbergh and among the first Americans to fly across the continent. On July 17, 1938 he climbed into his small plane and took off from Brooklyn on his way to Los Angeles. Twenty-six hours later he landed. At Baldonnel Field near Dublin, Ireland. He claimed he was confused and that his compass broke. In Ireland, "Wrong Way Corrigan" got a hero's welcome and even met the Irish prime minister. In London, U.S. Ambassador Joseph P. Kennedy embraced him, and upon his return to the United States (via boat), Corrigan was greeted with a ticker-tape parade. More than a million people lined the streets, more than had turned out for Lindbergh twelve years before. The cover of the *New York Post* announced: HAIL TO WRONG WAY CORRIGAN!—with the letters backward!

Today our congressmen routinely march in parades, sit at the best tables at restaurants and get reelected 90 percent of the time. It does not matter that they are flying our country in the wrong direction. Joseph Kennedy's son Teddy is happy to embrace them for these job-robbing policies. Dubliners would be happy to cheer them, too, just as they cheered Corrigan. Today hundreds of thousands of Irish workers hold outsourced jobs from more than one thousand global firms, including Dell, Pfizer and Citibank.

Attitude over Latitude

Most people, including many professional economists, think about a country's economy like a potential home buyer thinks about a model home. It's awfully hot in Panama! How lucky that Venezuela has oil! Too bad Australia is so far away from the action! The cliché "Location, location, location" might work well for buying a three-bedroom colonial in Peoria, but it's hardly worth a hill of beans when analyzing a country. Take Mexico, please. Mexico has enjoyed a great location, right on the U.S. border. It hasn't moved. Yet America's wealth and technology have not rubbed off much. Now look at prosperous Australia—a twelve-hour flight even after you change planes at LAX! And settled by criminals who sailed on leaky boats!

Economic textbooks waste a lot of time focusing on "factor endowments," telling us that a country blessed with lots of minerals and natural resources has a big advantage. Really? Hong Kong is a pile of rocks. The Netherlands was a sinking Venice but without the charming bridges or the spumoni, and yet in the seventeenth century she leapfrogged her better endowed neighbors. And then there's Israel today. She may be settled by God's chosen people but He chose not to give them a drop of oil, while gushers spout across Arabia. Did you ever read Mark Twain's description of the arid and empty land? Israel's terrain doesn't naturally grow enough green for a sprig of parsley on your dinner plate, and yet there she blooms. In the race for economic development would you rather bet on a country with a million tons of endowed zinc or one with a couple extra IQ points and a free flow of ideas?

A big endowment of riches may even be a curse. The earth under many parts of Africa bulges with metals. And yet the economies are retarded as oligarchs hang on to power, preventing capital from diffusing through society. Think back to the schoolbook atlases that displayed the natural resources of each country. As a kid, I always thought it unfair that the evil Soviet Union seemed to have all the great stuff, even bauxite, which sounded like a mysterious, earthly version of kryptonite, a bad thing in an enemy's arsenal. But the Soviet system had a reverse Midas touch. It turned precious metals and rich soil into famine and poverty. Way back in 1300 when Yuan dynasty vases were being baked, the Chinese had all the technology they needed to beat England to the Industrial Revolution. But the mandarins of the time stomped on trade and financial flows.[2] Because leftists refused to believe that "attitude beats latitude," they felt sorry and made excuses for the Soviet Union's seventy years of bad weather. As Ronald Reagan put it, there are just four things wrong with Communist farming: "winter, spring, summer, and fall."

What counts most, then? *Attitude, not latitude.* And here's where America is headed for trouble. What is America's attitude toward taxing corporations? Admitting skilled immigrants? Educating our children? Dragging one another into court? Rather than tarring and feathering corporate bigwigs, we must tear down the obstacles to a stronger economy. This book will show that outsourcing makes a great deal of economic sense—*given the current condition of the U.S. education system and job market. However, outsourcing may be a warning sign, a symptom, of our economic and educational failures, which should provoke us to reform.* We should not blame Citibank for hiring Filipino telemarketers when U.S. high schools grant diplomas to so many illiterate young people. We should not blame Motorola for hiring

Russian software writers when so many Americans opt out of mathematics and computer science after their sophomore year of high school.

In the ancient world, more soldiers and slaves meant more wealth. In the Middle Ages, the world depended on raw materials—which country could best mine iron ore or grow wheat. By 1700, countries that mastered shipping lanes were winning the race. By 1850, those that organized factories and blue-collar laborers moved ahead. Today, though, only those firms and countries that promote intelligence will survive and thrive. In the twenty-first century, IQ points are the new Dow Jones points. Simply put, whichever country deploys the most IQ points generates the most growth. This is a fundamental shift. Scroll back through Wall Street history and you'll find brawny, muscular names like Tennessee Coal and Iron; Distilling and Cattle Feeding Company; U.S. Leather. Now our hopes ride with, for example, the software writers at Microsoft, the scientists at Merck and the financial innovators at Bank of America. Not all of these companies are new, of course. Bank of America got off the ground during the earthquake and fires of San Francisco in 1906 when an Italian immigrant set up two planks on a wharf and started loaning desperately needed cash.[3] Compared with the early twentieth century, the American economy needs more scientists, engineers and financial experts, not more forklift drivers. Anybody left driving a forklift must be very familiar with logistical software. Our current immigration rules are perfectly suited for the economy of 1906.

We are in a race for intelligent workers but let's be honest. Not everyone has the capacity to understand higher chemistry. However, it is clear that we are failing to motivate our most gifted and giving up too soon on our lower achievers. Our monopoly public schools focus mostly on the "middle," but perhaps the word "muddle" better describes the results. Over the centuries, the U.S. economy has shifted from relying literally on horsepower to the engineered horsepower of machines to the brainpower that discovers, creates and refines software algorithms, pharmaceutical formulae, and entertainment media. Brainpower shows up, not just in the flashiest new camera phones but in old-fashioned products, too, like cows. When I last visited Iowa, I learned that cows have bar codes. Why? So that when a cow trudges in for feeding, she receives the right mix of feed grain to optimize her milk output. We deploy technology everywhere. Today even if you drive an eleven-thousand-dollar Chevy Cavalier, there is more computing power under the hood than in the Apollo rocket that brought Neil Armstrong to the moon in 1969. The United States needs a workforce with critical thinking skills. Other countries have already figured this out. Even if we outsource dull, repetitive assembly-line jobs, the United States should be hanging on to the brainpower jobs.

Imagine two distinct, famous images: the bulging bicep of the Arm & Hammer logo and Mickey Mouse. The Arm & Hammer bicep first appeared in the 1860s, symbolizing an economy built on muscle and moving mass. In the early twentieth century the most impressive firms, like National Lead, made things that you would not want to drop on your foot. When Mickey Mouse's first movie, *Steamboat Willie,* debuted in 1928, the boat was worth far more than the sketch of the plucky mouse. But by mid-century things were changing. The twentieth century began to sparkle with imagination, and value came from weightless stuff like streaming electrons, wireless phones and imaginary characters instantly recognized throughout the world. In contrast to the "heavy" economy of the nineteenth century, our economy's value comes from the human mind, not just from gritty, heavy stuff we mined from the ground.

Whenever a new *Harry Potter* or *Star Wars* movie comes out, devoted fans from Los Angeles to Kuala Lumpur sleep on lawn chairs and cots in front of theaters so that they can get tickets for the premier. I met a man who was so fanatically fascinated with astronauts and outer space that he stood on a two-foot cement block for twenty-four hours in order to win a contest to eat lunch with *Star Wars* director George Lucas. One hopes they served the man more than Tang. Lucas's movies have raked in several billion dollars, which would buy a lot of boxes of baking soda. The key is that Lucas did not create several billion dollars of value based on the weight of the celluloid film reel or of the DVDs. Instead, his *ideas* and technology mesmerized viewers who were willing to pay for an experience.

We can tally the value of some ideas by adding up the sales of copyrighted and trademarked materials. What kind of industries rely on copyrights? Books, software, films, TV programs, videos, DVDs and music recordings. Together these copyright industries create more than half a trillion dollars of value, more than 5 percent of the U.S. economy. As of 2001, almost five million Americans made their livings developing and marketing copyright materials—double the number in 1977.[4] Just walk into any bookstore and you will see shelves of magazines devoted to computers and entertainment. The magazines themselves, as well as the industries they cover, represent a tidal wave of creativity. The United States has a spectacular story to tell on copyrighted exports, too, which total about one hundred billion dollars annually. You would not get so high a number even if you stacked up our exported planes, trains, automobiles, corned beef and cabbage. Yet many of these jobs will vanish unless we act.

Roadblocks and Blockheads

Imagine going to a job interview with a sign posted on your back that reads, I'M VERY EXPENSIVE AND REALLY DON'T KNOW MUCH. That's the disadvantage leftist policies foist on American job candidates when they are competing with foreigners. In the chapters that follow I will expose the policy blunders that distort and disadvantage American workers, persuading employers to find offshore outsourcing more and more attractive:

Enormous Litigation Costs: Foreign outsourced workers do not sue. Lawsuits cut the U.S. GDP (gross domestic product) by more than 2 percent, while trial lawyers collect twenty-five billion dollars each year. Company managers often refuse to give references anymore, fearing they will be dragged into court by a disgruntled former employee.

Education: Foreign outsourced workers can calculate more than just their blood alcohol level after a keg party. Our twelfth graders know a lot less than Slovenians and just manage to beat out South Africa and Cyprus in math and science. Chinese engineering students outnumber Americans three to one. Even poor Russia, with half the U.S. population, educates 30 percent more engineers.

Taxation: The United States piles tax after tax on top of an employee's wage, so that a cheap worker costs big bucks. Virtually no one trusts Social Security and Medicare, but the fear of ever higher taxes persuades businesses to hire foreigners.

Barriers to Entry: Regulators and unions keep out competitors by erecting ludicrous hurdles, including licensing requirements and silly tests. Nearly one-fifth of jobs require a license, even to arrange flowers in Louisiana or fix a VCR in New York.

Immigration: We push away highly skilled foreigners who would launch new American companies and instead invite the old, the unskilled and the dependent. Indian and Chinese CEOs launch one-quarter of Silicon Valley firms, but our laws discourage them from creating jobs for Americans.

That's Entertainment?: We miss enormous opportunities to export American entertainment products because the entertainment industry is tone deaf to foreign cultures. Peru can export soap operas to Russia, but U.S. shows are banned in Beijing.

If we do not reform these areas dramatically and soon, the United States will morph from a high-powered economy into a "lip-synching economy." In the lip-synching economy, we still go to work, but we merely go through the motions while producing less and less and exerting only a whisper's impact as the world economy roars ahead.

Outsourcing: Who? What? Where? Why? How Much?

Intel just hired Dmitri, a computer programmer in Nizhni Novgorod. You could tap into Dmitri's telephone calls or the telephone calls of his new boss and still not know the answer to the following questions: Was he hired to replace David, an American in Santa Clara? Was he hired to help Intel penetrate the Russian market? Was he hired to help develop software that will be loaded onto new computers built in Austin, Texas, Taipei or Prague? It is awfully tough to measure the impact of outsourcing simply by counting up the number of foreign people employed by big U.S. companies. Even if you could tally the numbers you would miss the smaller firms that do not report layoffs to the federal government. The front page of the *Wall Street Journal* reported that while union contracts prevent the Big Three automakers from offshore outsourcing, the carmakers are simply forcing their suppliers to do so.[5] The article reported that Chinese parts quintupled to one billion dollars between 1997 and 2003. Now let's say that cheap Chinese parts allow GM to cut the prices of a Buick, inducing more Americans to stroll into the showrooms. Perhaps that would lead to more jobs in Detroit. Again, I am in favor of free trade.[6] But I fear that stupid rules, regulations and taxes are pressuring firms to hire fewer Americans than they otherwise would.

I first noticed the new outsourcing wave about four years ago while lecturing to technology executives. During coffee breaks, white-collar jobholders with frown lines on their faces began to pepper me with worries about their new "partners" in Bangalore and Beijing. I began speaking with CEOs and COOs, who confessed that their new hires were largely abroad. They might not be firing Americans, but they were not looking to hire more here. India, Ireland, Israel and China seemed to be nabbing the new jobs. Irish and Israeli programmers earned half as much as Americans while Indians and Chinese worked for one-quarter the salary. Estimating the number of outsourced jobs has been like staring at a dusty, scratchy crystal ball. After interviewing a few thousand executives, vendors and customers, Forrester Research states that more than 800,000 white-collar jobs will travel offshore by 2005 and 3.4 million by 2015. Researchers at the University of California's, Berkeley, Haas School of Business believe that Forrester is too conservative and that 14 million jobholders should be trembling.[7] Between 1999 and 2001, data entry jobs dropped by 115,000, or 22 percent, before the 2001 recession began to bite. A real estate firm based in Chicago interviewed forty leading companies and concluded that 80 percent of their real estate executives expected to expand their offshore call centers and computer services over the next five years, with 42.5 percent actually transferring U.S. jobs overseas.[8] The anecdotes are certainly piling up high as suburban real estate firms fret about see-through offices in the United States. Consultants at Ernst & Young are divulging to clients that 50 million square feet of office space will be wasted.[9]

Optimists reply that multinationals have created more U.S. jobs than they have destroyed.[10] A popular rhetorical rebuttal to outsourcing is "insourcing"; that is, foreign companies hiring Americans. More than six million Americans already work for foreign firms, and the number is climbing. Samsung is expanding its Austin semiconductor plant; Swiss drug company Novartis is buying beakers and test tubes for its new research facility in Cambridge, Massachusetts. San Antonio cowboys may soon be doing jumping jacks in front of a spanking new Toyota pickup truck plant. Republicans have gleefully reported that the Heinz Company owns fifty-seven plants all around the world, which benefits many workers, customers and shareholders, including John Kerry and his wife. This is entertaining and mostly good news. But such stories do not actually prove how outsourcing itself creates more U.S. jobs, nor do they assess how many jobs are lost through policy blunders in the United States. Eventually, higher wages in Asia may slow down the pace of outsourcing, but today that comforting thought seems far away and far afield.

Rather than unveil my own crystal ball to forecast the numbers of outsourced jobs and empty floor space, this book focuses on the dreadful policy mistakes that cost us jobs. We could handle "losing" 3.4 million, or even 14 million, outsourced jobs to the developing world if we did not punish firms for hiring Americans here and if we did not put such high hurdles in front of young workers trying to find their way into a decent job.

Which jobs are most vulnerable? Let's relieve your tension about at least one thing. Your barber or hair stylist will not be outsourced. People you must see "face-to-face" or "scissors to head" won't leave you. Outsourced jobs generally rely on telecommunications, use a lot of information and do not require much social networking. A friend of mine is a radiologist. A few years ago, when the victim of a midnight car accident got rushed to the ER, he would rush to the hospital in his pajamas to look at the X-rays. Now he rolls over in bed as the hospital zaps the chart electronically to Nighthawk Radiology in Sydney, Australia. You've heard of I. M. Pei and Philip Johnson. How about Balazs Zimay? He's a very busy Budapest architect who will design your house for one-third the price of an American firm. Are you an inventor in need of a patent? I hold several engineering and design patents and have paid tens of thousands of dollars to a U.S. law firm to file them with the Patent and Trademark Office. Now, highly trained patent attorneys offshore can write the applications just as effectively and much less expensively, giving inventors a head start on their ventures.

Each outsourcing destination has different characteristics. Let's briefly discuss three. Why does India grab more headlines? India grabs the most attention and the most revenue because of its awesome supply of highly educated, computer-literate professionals. Last year India earned about $14 billion by handling business processes and designing techonologies. Giant firms like

Wipro, Infosys and Cognizant (a spin-off of Dun & Bradstreet) have proved to American customers that the Indians can deliver on time and with a high degree of accuracy. HiTech City, a Flash Gordon area of the four-hundred-year-old city of Hyderabad, juxtaposes ancient monuments and space-age architecture. Microsoft, Oracle, GE Capital and Toshiba all feel right at home; software exports from HiTech City reached nearly $1.5 billion last year. In 2004 some pundits worried about political unrest in India when the people threw out the Hindu nationalist Bharatiya Janata Party. But the left-leaning Congress Party immediately tapped as prime minister a pro-trade, pro-globalization former finance minister, Manmohan Singh. So whether it goes slightly left or slightly right, India is not looking to go backward to its disastrous Socialist past.

The Philippines offers a less tech-savvy, though very efficient home for call centers. I learned about Filipino outsourcing by first driving to Monrovia. Not in Liberia, but a suburban town east of Los Angeles. In an office decorated with Asian paintings, sculpture and art, two former McKinsey executives run a dynamic business called e-Telecare, employing thousands of Filipinos at call centers in Manila. Why Manila? Copresidents Derek Holley and Jim Franke explained that the Filipino workforce speaks English fluently, shows up on time and is half as likely to quit in the middle of the year as Americans at a U.S.-based call center. "It's a performance-based culture. We hire only people with college degrees. And we can reward individuals for strong performance, without worrying about union complaints," says Holley calmly. When the Philippines deregulated telecommunications costs fell 90 percent; e-Telecare pays just a few pennies a minute to route a call from, say, Kalamazoo, Michigan, through their Monrovia offices to Manila.[11] Filipino workers may not offer the technological sophistication of Indian engineers, he admits, but they are more culturally friendly to Americans. "They love the NBA!" he reports.

The outsourcing business has been so lucrative that even Barbados now competes for the action! Why Barbados? A company called IMA hires locals to work out of a seventy-five-hundred square-foot call center in Bridgetown. In addition to low attrition and low costs, IMA boasts that the Barbados accent is an "excellent fit" for both USA and UK customers. Fodor's labels the predominant "Bajan accent" as a "hybrid Irish lilt!"[12] Bully, bully!

Outsourcing often saves time and money, but sometimes fails, too, when cultures clash on the telephone or in the boardroom. American executives have learned that outsourcing may falter when they change their minds or change their work orders too frequently. A Bangalore programmer may cost much less than a Pittsburgh programmer, but if you have to fly the Indian halfway across the world for tutorials, any cost savings will evaporate. The frequent flier miles are not worth the hassle. Nonetheless, when you consider the massive job orders being beamed each day from the United States to Asia, outsourcing must be generating many more fans than detractors in the corner offices.

Can America Compete?

Can America compete? Of course. But we need to tear off those dastardly labels pinned to our jackets that declare I'M VERY EXPENSIVE AND REALLY DON'T KNOW MUCH. American workers will not succeed *because* of the government but *in spite of* the government. Regardless of the treacherous roadblocks in front of us, the American people still buzz with creativity. In the American DNA swirls a gene for audacity and courage. And, miraculously, even if you are not born here, that gene sneaks under your skin when you pass the Statue of Liberty. Despite all the sharp lawyers, nasty tax collectors and dull school bureaucrats, this is still the place where entrepreneurs can most easily raise money and raise hell for competitors. Though the popular press will portray China, India, Mexico and all the others as predators trying to steal our jobs, leaving us with just a drawer full of pink slips, in truth, we are stealing from ourselves. It's time to go straight. We have the world to gain, and nothing to lose but our chains.

TWO

Silicon, Soy and Curry

How Immigration Laws Thwart U.S. Growth

Take a look at your hands. What do you see? Clipped nails and soft skin smoothed by moisturizing soaps and lotions? Then get back on the boat and go home. That's the message you would have heard if you had tried to come to the United States in the 1800s. Were Americans discriminating against cleanliness? No. But they were looking for calluses and scars, unmistakable signs that the hands knew how to work hard in an agrarian economy. America needed manual laborers to hammer nails and harvest wheat, not academics or soft-skinned metrosexuals. In 1850, bustling New York City housed only three hundred thousand people. Sixty percent of Americans worked on the farms, whether in the emerging corn belt of Iowa or a few miles uptown in the Bronx. So naturally the country prized bulging biceps and strong backs over the ability to solve differential equations.

Consider the horse. In the 1850s horses found a welcoming job market. Whether on rural lands or in cities, horses could pull carriages, haul ice or lug carts loaded with coal. They provided brawn, not necessarily brains. Imagine you are a horse today, sitting on your sofa in pajamas staring at the Help-wanted ads in the Sunday paper. You won't find many opportunities. Did horses get fat, lazy and feckless over the past 150 years? They can still outrun a man and might even outrun a car stuck in grid-locked traffic. But our modern economy creates few opportunities for them, outside of trotting tourists through Central Park or posing on a Christmas card from Anheuser-Busch breweries. Our economy demands brains, critical thinking and finely honed skills. There's little room for horses.

Unfortunately, our immigration policies have been stuck in the past, willfully ignorant. Our laws and regulations not only ignore the pressing need for more skills and intellect; they also deliberately chase away those talented people who could most help the United States survive the grinding pressures of baby boom retirement. So dumb are our laws and rules, you might think they were legislated by the horses that run in the Kentucky Derby instead of the people who win congressional races.

In 1920, nobody told immigrants what to sell, and nobody provided them with bilingual education. The comedian Billy Crystal jokes that his grandfather came to America at the age of nine, got a pushcart and started pushing it up and down the streets of New York. At nine and a half he realized, "Schmuck! Put something in the empty cart and start selling." In seventy-five years the economy has moved from pushcarts to PalmPilots. What are today's immigrants selling? For the most part, they are pushing empty pushcarts and have only calluses to sell. Why? Surely, there are millions of smart, highly trained Mexicans, Indians, Zimbabweans and Filipinos who would love to live in the United States and eventually become citizens. Quite simply, we don't ask. Our immigration policies hardly care whether newcomers have the potential to cure breast cancer or the potential merely to show their chest at a strip club. Only about 10 percent of U.S. immigrants arrive because they have qualified under the convoluted provisions for skilled workers. The overwhelming number (about 75 percent) arrive under the "family reunification" principle, exalted in the 1965 Immigration and Nationality Acts Amendments. The phrase sounds almost incontrovertibly comfortable and would seem to slip easily among "baseball, hot dogs, apple pie and Chevrolet." Yet the mathematics behind family reunification are explosive and exponential. Assume that Dick and Liz—born anywhere you choose—come to the United States and become naturalized citizens. Soon, their brothers and sisters arrive under sponsorship preferences, along with their spouses. Then come the children, along with the elderly parents. Have you ever stood patiently in line for a ride at Disney World and been asked to make room for another person, not realizing that the other person was actually a party of twelve? Welcome to the immigration line for the United States. No wonder, then, that family ties dominate and nearly exclude other categories. Shouldn't U.S. policy makers at least ask whether mama, papa, grandma and grandpa will be requiring government assistance?

Funny enough, the sponsors of the 1965 legislation, led by President Lyndon Johnson and Senators Ted and Robert F. Kennedy, assured the American public that the amendments would not significantly shake up the mathematics. Senator Robert F. Kennedy told readers of the *New York Times* that the old system would be "replaced by the merit system" and that we would not be "deprive[d] of able immigrants whose contributions we need."[1] Senator Ted Kennedy told worried senators that "our cities will not be flooded with a million immigrants annually. . . . The bill will not upset the ethnic mix of our society. It will not relax the standards of admission."[2] The Kennedys have claimed many successes and talents. But they've never claimed superior mathematical skills. Since 1965 a chart of immigration levels shows a sharp upward slope, from around three hundred thousand per year to roughly a million by the mid-1990s.

Chasing Away Talent

My argument with the Kennedys is not about whether the United States should have permitted more immigration over the past forty years. There's a more important point: Robert F. Kennedy's assurances about "merit" and "contributions" have missed the mark by millions of people and billions of dollars in wages and profits that could have been generated by talented would-be immigrants who were turned away. If Albert Einstein showed up at the borders today, most bureaucrats would care less about his brain than about photos of his grandkids and brother-in-law to prove his family ties.

To bring jobs home to the United States, the United States needs a system that brings the most able people to America. We commit two mistakes. First, we do too little to entice skilled people to come to the United States. Second, we actually chase away smart people who could add to our national culture, national spirit and, yes, national wealth. Simply put: educated and skilled immigrants drive up our GDP and our standard of living.

Too much of our bitter national debate on immigration has surrounded the costs and benefits of admitting uneducated, unskilled people. It's hard to tease out clear conclusions from the statistics, though Harvard's George Borjas will tell you that immigrants cost the economy dearly, and his critics, like Michael Fix at the Urban Institute, will tell you that Borjas is flat wrong.[3] As I discuss below, President Bush's 2004 proposal added to this furor by focusing on the jobs "Americans will not do." Supporters of unskilled immigrants, whether legal or illegal, ask, "Who will pick strawberries, mow lawns or wash dishes in the restaurants?" Quite honestly, I don't think the future of our economy depends on busboys and leaf blowers. The whole immigration debate should be flipped on its head. Rather than attracting millions of uneducated people, the United States should pry open the legal gates to recruit many more educated, skilled people, whether from Mexico, China or Ghana.

No one I know disputes that admitting intelligent, educated or skilled non-Americans will expand our national pie. Why? America gets the benefit of their brainpower and training, but we don't foot the bill for their birth, early health care or schooling. The National Academy of Sciences estimates that a college-educated immigrant who shows up on our shores delivers a +$198,000 impact on our fiscal picture, paying far more in taxes than he receives in social spending. His cousin with less than a high school education costs other taxpayers about $13,000.[4] Now imagine the opportunity cost: taking in one hundred thousand college grads instead of high school dropouts would generate an additional $21 billion over their lifetimes. Even small adjustments in the roughly million people the United States takes in each year could reshape the fiscal picture of our most populous states.

Again, you do not have to take a negative view of uneducated immigrants to see the difference. Even if you assume (heroically and optimistically) that high school dropout immigrants have a small positive fiscal impact, there is no question that their well-educated brethren bring more to our table, literally and figuratively.

Liberal immigration advocates cannot deny this point. The

American Immigration Law Foundation states that "a better educated populace earns more, pays more taxes and has less need for public health."[5] Its solution: invite in more unskilled, uneducated people, but educate them here, at U.S. taxpayer expense.

Pavel is a cardiac researcher in Prague. Though in the precommunism era, many of his uncles and relatives were doctors, his cousins and siblings could not persuade the Communist bosses to let them study medicine. Pavel persevered, though, and finally graduated from Charles University. Despite the obstacles of communism he managed to fight his way into the most challenging areas of research involving the use of ultraviolet light to detect the risk of stroke. After the velvet revolution, he set up a successful private practice in cardiology. A few years ago he earned a fellowship to one of the most advanced laboratories in the University of California system. He left his wife and three kids behind to pursue his science. After completing a six-month term in the United States, he packed his bags to return home. Though his research may some day save your life, there was no room for him under our convoluted and twisted system. Today he toils at a lab in Prague. Meanwhile, the man who trimmed the shrubs in front of Pavel's San Diego apartment maneuvers to bring his parents into the country.

Most educated or skilled people who do navigate their way through an unwelcoming system come either under student visas or the H-1B program for "specialty occupations" and professions. To get a student visa, the student stands in line at the U.S. Embassy in a foreign country and begs for the mercy of local bureaucrats. Sharon C. is a determined twenty-two-year-old who is used to making her own way. She grew up on a Zimbabwe cattle ranch, far from the comforts of the upper classes. She waited for nine hours in front of the U.S. Embassy in Harare, the corrupt capital of Robert Mugabe's fiefdom. She wanted to study early child development in the United States. While the U.S. Embassy is led by Americans, they hire locals to staff the administrative offices. A white woman who lives with her widowed mother and two younger brothers, Sharon wondered whether her skin color explained the brusque reception she felt. More likely it was simply the color-blind lethargy of bureaucrats. After sweating in the 90 degree heat for nine hours, the windows closed and she was sent away. She quickly arranged to stay at a hostel, because her home was too far away. The next day she returned, standing for five hours until she finally reached an interviewer. Did they care much about her studies? Her grades? Her letters of recommendation, attesting to her intelligence? No. What was most important? That she solemnly swear that she would leave the United States after her studies and that she had money tied up in Zimbabwe and a mother who needed her to return. The more dire the home situation the better. The most attractive candidate would have a sick parent, a house in urgent need of repair and a stash of foreign-denominated money that the government could keep an eye on. And remember, this is the U.S. Embassy! What's the logic here? We attract smart people from throughout the world, help expand their minds and then kick them out—rather than inviting them to stay, which would make America healthier, wealthier and wiser. When these keen people return home, they are smart, fluent and conversant with U.S. culture. In other words, perfectly suited to handle outsourcing jobs.

For a foreign professional to enter the United States on an H-1B visa (currently limited to sixty-five thousand, though it had been about two hundred thousand a few years ago) an employer must attest to his special skills and pay the prevailing U.S. wage. But a loud clock ticks in the background. He may stay for three years, which might be extended for another three. And then, like Cinderella at midnight, the professional must race down the steps and hit the road, or the docks, or the tarmac, under the threat of arrest.

What does the foreign professional do after returning home? He, too, becomes an ideal candidate for outsourcing. The more entrepreneurial types will start their own businesses, deploying the tools they learned while working in the United States.

Does this make any sense? These people are mobile, global assets. In many cases we should entice them to become mobile, global, American assets. The visa system becomes even more infuriating when you learn that the process is essentially "first come, first served." In February 2004, the Homeland Security Department announced that all sixty-five thousand H-1B visa slots had been filled for the year. No point in recruiting anyone else till next year, no matter how gifted or how valuable she might be to a company or to the U.S. economy.

Ingersoll-Rand Company boasts that it runs manufacturing plants in twenty-four states. With 120 facilities come thousands of job descriptions for specialized skills. "We must be able to tap the talent we need. . . . When Human Resource Managers cannot fill key positions with workers from the domestic workforce, *they are forced to look outside the U.S. to hire or outsource the work* [italics added]," stated their director of immigration services before the U.S. Senate.[6] A stingy quota combined with a perverse immigration system nearly push such firms offshore.

Some critics of student and H-1B visas argue that they take American slots at colleges, laboratories and corporate offices. Rather than try to convert them to potential citizenship, they would lock the door and prevent them from ever coming over. Let's take each program separately. As I argue in Chapter 3, we are in a race for skills and intelligence. Today, only about 50 percent to 60 percent of our high-tech graduate degrees go to Americans. This is not just a U.S. phenomenon; the Brits can relate. When I attended graduate school at Cambridge University in the 1980s, my econometrics class was taught by an Iranian and the strongest student was a Zimbabwean. United States colleges will award about 61,000 undergraduate degrees in engineering this year, compared with 195,000 in China, 129,000 in India and 103,000 in Japan. Even if our degree standards are more rigorous, we should not ignore the hundreds of thousands of engineering graduates who could help us boost our standard of living. When they come here as graduate students they tend not to displace native Americans. Few highly intelligent, hardworking, newly minted electrical engineering B.S.s fail to find a graduate post.

Note one more advantage of admitting foreign students: they tend to pay for it, which generates more cash for our colleges. Further, it counts as a U.S. export. An Irish kid working in the physics lab of MIT is a U.S. export to Ireland, just as an Irish tourist to the Grand Canyon counts as an American export.

The business world similarly needs the brainpower. Technology businesses seek brain cells like cats seek tuna. And like cats, these businesses won't be bothered much by what brand or nationality shows up on the table. Joseph Costello, former CEO of Cadence Design Systems of San Jose asserts that "high tech is blind to the concept of 'immigrant' . . . [American engineers] are competing with every other engineer in the entire world and it's an ultimate test: do your skills stand up?"[7] Back in 1996, long before the outsourcing outcry, Cadence employed thirty-two hundred people, only 40 percent of them American.

Bill Gates may be color-blind. Judging by his shirts I'd guess so. But Gates is most certainly color-blind in his hiring. Brainpower trumps all. "There is no way of getting around [the fact] that, in terms of IQ, you've got to be elitist in picking people to write software." He admitted his hiring bias "toward intelligence or smartness over anything else, even, in many cases, experience." [8] Does it make sense for Gates to hire people, only to send them packing in a few years?

Consider Andy Grove, cofounder and former CEO of Intel. Surely, developing and then leading the world's greatest chip-making firm was a challenge demanding brilliance, patience and pluck. But here was a Hungarian-born scientist named Grf Andrs who first had to survive the Nazis and then the wicked Soviet invasion in 1956. No wonder he named his biography *Only the Paranoid Survive*. If not for Andy Grove, there might not be an INTEL INSIDE sticker on your computer, and America's dominance of advanced semiconductors might have flickered and displayed a FATAL ERROR message. Do we want an immigration system that increases or decreases the chances that the next Andy Grove lands on our shores—and stays?

Ten years ago, the United States could afford to arrogantly swagger and declare not just that the United States was the land of opportunity, but also that it was just about the only land of opportunity. President Clinton toured the world boasting of U.S. business genius and financial superiority. (This was before the economy slid into recession and the NASDAQ plunged from about 5,000 to 1,500.) Now the world has changed. Other countries like India and China have shed many of their Socialist regulations and have opened up lucrative opportunities for their citizens. Naveed Sherwani, a former Intel executive, has just opened up a chip-design center in India called Open-Silicon Inc. Smart non-Americans now get job offers at home. In 1985 Taiwan established a venture capital industry and launched the Hsinchu Science-Based Industrial Park. Over half the companies in the park have been started by Silicon Valley returnees.

For most of the post–World War II era, the United States enjoyed a captive audience among scientists and engineers in the developing world. Few would turn down an American job or fellowship. Few would leave early, until forced home by our silly laws and regulations. Now they have choices. The test tubes and mainframes at U.S. laboratories and design plants may not be so superior to those found elsewhere. There is no guarantee that the formerly captive audience will stay. In fact, they appear to be packing their bags sooner. In 1996, more than twenty-five hundred Chinese science and engineering doctoral graduates intended to stay in the United States. Three years later that number dropped by about 25 percent.[9] About three-quarters of Silicon Valley's immigrants report that they would consider starting businesses in their native countries. Just as Shanghai beckons, American policy says "Good riddance."

Educated Immigrants Create Jobs

Union leaders and liberal politicians respond to educated immigrants like the Wicked Witch does to water: "I'm melting." They worry that their roles will be diminished, and they scream about job displacement. What they do not say is that educated immigrants are more entrepreneurial and far more likely to create new jobs than cost old jobs. How many jobs has Andy Grove created? The Hungarian-born billionaire financier George Soros has created many jobs—most recently for left-wing fund-raisers. How many dancers owe their careers to a pirouette and plié taught by George Ballanchine?

In Silicon Valley, the entrepreneurial spirit of Indian and Chinese immigrants has been displayed with awesome results. According to one respected survey, 51 percent of immigrants have been involved in founding or running a start-up company. And it didn't take them long. Most of these respondents had been in the country less than ten years! Almost two-thirds said they intended to start their own companies—a pretty ambitious attitude considering they filled out the survey during the bloody "tech wreck" of 2001, a terrible time to raise new capital.[10]

Are these hookah dreams? Apparently not. Indian and Chinese rates of going public are similar to companies led by U.S. natives. Dun & Bradstreet reported that Indian and Chinese engineers were running one-quarter of Silicon Valley firms in 1998, accounting for almost seventeen billion dollars in sales and more than fifty-eight thousand jobs! The spirit of entrepreneurship has been infectious. Indian and Chinese CEOs were running 13 percent of Silicon Valley tech firms in the early 1980s, but almost one-third by 2000. Do the fifty-eight thousand jobholders feel aggrieved by this can-do fury?

What about those foreign workers who enter on H-1B visas and do not try to start new firms? Do they push down the wages of native Americans? The Federal Reserve Bank of Atlanta conducted a study in 2003 and failed to find a negative impact on U.S. wages. After all, the visiting workers were more highly educated than typical Americans, earning almost 15 percent more than similar U.S. workers.[11] These were not bargain-basement window washers shipped over on leaky ferries. Even if foreign skilled workers were cheap, it is not cheap to get them here. An employer typically pays about two thousand dollars in legal fees, a thousand-dollar training/scholarship fee, and a thousand-dollar processing fee to the government. Of course, that does not include airfare, housing or other costs picked up by a company's human resources budget. A National Academy of Sciences and National Academy on Engineering report also found that foreign-born scientists earn significantly more on average than native scientists. Computer engineers are not stupid, whether they are born in Boise or Botswana. If they come here to design semiconductor chips, they won't accept payment in potato chips; they demand lots of cash.

Bamboo Networks

Welcoming highly skilled people offers yet another advantage: the United States can better tap into their networks. I don't mean telephone networks or Ethernets. I mean good, old-fashioned talking, jabbering and scheming to invent the better mousetrap. Despite the amazing speed with which electrons zap across our high-tech gadgets and gizmos, business deals often still come down to a handshake and a conversation. Our toys have evolved over the centuries, but human beings are still human beings. Venture capital firms ultimately place their bets not just on the quality of the technology but on their assessment of the team members; that is, their intellect, organizational skills and drive. It's hard to reduce these soft variables to a slide presentation with crisp bar graphs and pie charts. Over time, we found many industries dominated or at least heavily influenced by ethnic networks. The reasons are many and so are the examples. Often they lend themselves to stereotypes, such as the Irish cop, the Italian fashion designer, the Dominican shortstop. There's no denying, though, that if Alex Rodriguez urges a baseball scout to visit his cousin in Santo Domingo, the scout will hop on the next plane from JFK. Back in the 1950s and 1960s, a Jewish comedian in the borscht belt (Catskill Mountains) or Las Vegas could pave the way for another. Just ask David Brenner, who says that Buddy Hackett's recommendations got him out of the small lounges and into the big showrooms.

In the United States as well as Canada, Chinese networks have played enormous roles in transporting knowledge and "deal flow" across continents. Call them bamboo networks, if you like, for like bamboo, they spread quickly and durably. One recent study found that ethnic Chinese networks have spurred nearly 60 percent of the increase in specialized trade between China and the West.[12] Once again U.S. policy makers and citizens face the following question: Do we want to be part of this global conversation or not? The wheeling and dealing of human networks is not illegal, immoral or even fattening. If our government policies take a machete to bamboo networks, those networks will simply sprout up in other countries, creating jobs for other people.

Leaf Blowers and Busboys

If you listened to the popular media, you would think the most important question on immigration is whether tighter standards would give us a shortage of busboys balancing plates in the kitchens of restaurants. In the 2004 "mockumentary" film *A Day Without a Mexican,* an Anglo restaurateur complains, "I had to wash a dish." I have nothing but admiration for hardworking people who legally cross borders to help their families. My heart is with the Statue of Liberty and the "huddled masses yearning to breathe free." Moreover, we are probably facing a worker shortage over the next thirty years.

And yet we should not let images of national icons blind us to reality. As Milton Friedman has said, open borders do not match well with a welfare state. Today our society provides welfare, schooling, medical care and other social services to just about anyone who manages to cross our borders. In some parts of California and Texas, a majority of public school children are the sons and daughters of illegal aliens, who may themselves be here illegally. A similar majority populates the birthing wards of numerous hospitals. In the first half of the twentieth century, people spoke of pulling themselves up by their own bootstraps. With a lavish social welfare system, the boots of unskilled immigrants (legal and illegal) need not even touch the ground.

It would be comforting to know that legal immigrants were providing a rich source of young, vigorous workers who will eventually earn good wages, pay taxes and help bail out the bankrupt Social Security and Medicare programs. But if that's what you want, you are looking at the wrong crowd. Before the family reunification principle reigned supreme, a typical immigrant was young, male, adventurous and determined to climb up the socioeconomic ladder. Today, the typical immigrant is not predominantly male and, more important, is older than the typical native. The proportion of immigrants over sixty-five exceeds the proportion of natives. They may be able to climb up the ladder, but they're more likely to be doing it in orthopedic shoes. Furthermore, immigrants over sixty-five are more than twice as likely as natives to depend on Supplemental Security Income, which sends checks to the elderly poor.

A further cost may come to unskilled natives. While highly

skilled immigrants and visa visitors do not drive down wages or job offers for natives, the unskilled probably do, by about 1 percentage point to 3 percentage points.[13] The unskilled are far less likely to start businesses, of course. When immigrants do start modest businesses, it is not a zero-sum game. It is an urban myth that Asian businesses (for example, Korean food markets in New York City) drive out black-owned small businesses. You can see the tension in Spike Lee's 1989 *Do the Right Thing* and in the 1993 Allen and Albert Hughes's *Menace II Society.* In *Menace,* a Korean grocer mutters a slur at a young black thug, who then shoots the grocer in the head, steals the surveillance video and watches the scene again and again, boasting to his friends. On a 1991 album the performer known as Ice Cube rapped "Black Korea." He speaks of "oriental one-penny-countin' motherf--kers" and warns "your little chop suey ass'll be a target." Korean shopkeepers must "pay respect to the black fist or we'll burn your store, right down to a crisp." Let's put aside the issue of whether Korean grocers dis black teens or whether blacks retaliate by stealing. For all the sweat, blood and celluloid wasted on the topic, cold statistics covering ninety-four metropolitan areas argue that Asian shopkeepers do not drive African American store owners out of business.

In sum, when we admit skilled immigrants or immigrants who demonstrate a knack for or interest in starting businesses, we open up to them the promise of the American dream—without erasing that promise from the minds of those born in the U.S.A. Entrepreneurs may chase after money, but in doing so they create more liberty. A friend of mine ran the U.S. Treasury Department's office in Albania soon after the black fog of a despotic, demented communism lifted in the early 1990s. Under the Orwellian despot Enver Hoxa, impoverished Albania had pursued a form of communism far more lethal than even Soviet Communism. To Hoxa the Soviet Union was candy-coated gumdrops. He turned his country into a prison camp gulag, where slave laborers dug for toxic chromium. My colleague's first advice to the new Albanian government, not entirely facetious: "Bring in some Chinese small businessmen. And some Jews wouldn't hurt either."

Bingo! and Other Visa Madness

Within the maze of immigration programs also sits a national lottery. Now, you may think that gambling is still illegal in some states, yet each year the U.S. State Department spins the wheel and picks fifty-five thousand lucky winners (among about ten million applicants) to receive green cards, giving them permanent residency. These cards are so coveted that in 1997 the country of Sierra Leone was rocked by antigovernment riots. Why? Thousands of green card lottery applications had been found floating in Freetown Harbor. The green card lottery is sometimes called the diversity lottery, because countries that have sent more than fifty thousand immigrants in the past five years are not eligible. So, Canadians, Brits, Chinese, Indians and Jamaicans, for example, need not apply this year.

Once again Senator Ted Kennedy took a leading role in immigration, developing the diversity lottery as a way to ensure more Irish entrants. This charge is not some right-wing anti-Teddy propaganda. *Boston Magazine* reported that when "Congress ran a lottery to hand out 40,000 new visas to applicants from 34 countries in 1991, two Massachusetts politicians—Senator Edward M. Kennedy and then-Congressman Brian Donnelly—led the efforts to set almost half of them aside exclusively for immigrants from just one place: Ireland."[14] That's why Washington politicians refer to the lottery as the Irish program. Despite Kennedy's intentions, though, in recent years Ireland has faired poorly in the lottery, nabbing far fewer green cards than even Algeria and Sudan.

What is the logic behind this program? I suppose it can be captured in the phrase "random acts of kindness." But what is the opportunity cost? If we are to open up fifty-five thousand new slots each year, why spin a wheel or toss the dice? Where is the moral justice in awarding green cards to the lucky? That's Vegas morals, not those of Jefferson and Adams. Since it is impossible to examine the moral worth of applicants, why not at least insist that they can enhance and strengthen the foundation of our society and economy? Rather than merely demanding that these random winners hold high school diplomas, why not insist that applicants have a trade, a college degree or an IQ over the world average?

I fear that Americans support a diversity lottery because we've been taught that the word "diversity" is always good in all things. I disagree. Diversity in musical tastes, diversity in political voices, diversity in appearance are good. We don't want a country of clones or Stepford wives. But we should not be fooled into thinking that diversity of all things is best. Do we want diversity in justice? In honesty? The University of Ohio has a diverse campus, but it does not seek felons, nor does it seek morons. Shouldn't our standards admitting immigrants and citizens be just as tight?

Look for the Union Label

Unions have been as tempest tossed as the huddled masses when it comes to immigration. For most of the nineteenth and twentieth centuries, they tried to nail and rivet big barriers to keep out newcomers from our borders. Leaders believed that more immigrants drove down wages and prospects for unionism. The word "scab" easily translated into German, Italian, Chinese, Polish or whatever other group threatened to undermine the collective bargaining agreement. In the 1870s, the heralded American Federation of Labor leader Samuel Gompers (an immigrant from England) literally put the union label on cigars to distinguish them from the stogies made by nonunion Chinese immigrants. Those who took the reins from Gompers followed his lead and supported various restrictions, including the Immigration Act of 1924, which sharply curtailed immigrants from Asia while favoring Northern and Western Europe over Southern and Eastern Europe. After World War II, the AFL supported President Truman's plan to temporarily ease restrictions, but the AFL saw this as a one-time favor to devastated European refugees.

A funny thing happened on the way to the twenty-first century, though. As union membership plunged in the last few decades, union leaders desperately sought new constituencies. Unskilled immigrants, who could join unions as dishwashers, bellmen, janitors and sanitation workers, began to look more attractive. At its convention in 1993, the AFL-CIO performed an about-face and embraced them, calling for a higher minimum wage, stricter working conditions and more universal health care. As the 1990s wore on, the AFL-CIO moved not just to embrace unskilled legal immigrants, but even illegal aliens. The union fought for amnesty for illegal aliens and to repeal the laws that allowed the government to fine those bosses who hired illegals.

Despite the AFL-CIO's performing an about-face on immigration, it seems to me that big labor has been wrong twice! Back in the nineteenth century when America needed the calloused hands of the unskilled, big labor tried to lock the doors. In our day, big labor wants to throw open the doors without any regard for the quality or legality of the entrants. Today immigrants arrive in the United States (legally and illegally) without anyone's seriously questioning whether they might ever find a job or pay a dime in income taxes over their lifetime. Big labor has played a big role in building the social welfare state. They should feel some responsibility to make sure that new citizens can afford to sustain it rather than drain it.

Brain Drain?

Am I advocating a brain drain for other countries? After all, I want the U.S. government to admit more immigrants, but insist that most have either high skills or high aptitude, as demonstrated in college degrees, college placement exams or even IQ tests. Will this cheat Mexico, India and, say, South Africa of their best and brightest?

Two responses. First, my purpose in this book is to address the perverse incentives built into U.S. policies and to raise the chances that the United States survives and thrives in this century. I would hope that the United States pursues its enlightened national interests. If not, we might as well trade in the Senate for the UN Security Council.

Second, and more surprising perhaps: I think the brain drain hypothesis is simplistic and often wrong. Remember the earlier discussion of ethnic networks? Well, it seems that skilled immigrants, especially in the sciences, frequently maintain and build out their personal and professional networks, which deliver insights and opportunities back to their home country. Even in an intellectual diaspora, a web connects expatriates. If you visit northern California, you might sit in on meetings of the Korean Scientists Engineering Association of Sacramento. Moreover, successful immigrants in the United States encourage those left behind to develop their skills. This supercharges the incentives and raises the rewards for personal investments in human capital.[15] A postcard or e-mail sent from the United States allows young people to see the value in schooling and training, which can push up the average level of knowledge in a developing country. The amazing economic progress in Shanghai and Bangalore has been encouraged and partly fueled by the amazing successes of Asians in America. Even Calcutta, often portrayed as a fetid place relieved only by the miracles of the late Mother Teresa, has been hosting technology start-ups and new shopping malls, dotted with cinemas and coffee bars. Forget clichéd worries about a brain drain; the reality is a cerebral circle of knowledge, sending ideas, money and business deals around the world.

Learning from Others

During the booming 1990s, guess which country followed the United States in launching the most high-tech companies? Japan? Germany? I'll give you a hint. It's a small place, just half the size of Switzerland. Mmm, you think it must be a trick question, like phantom money management firms in the Grand Caymans. No. The answer is Israel, home to thousands of cutting-edge labs and design plants. "Our country is one big laboratory," said Azriel Hemer, former deputy chief scientist at Israel's Department of Industry and Economics.[16] A key reason for Israel's high-tech prowess: eight hundred thousand Russian immigrants who fled from the former Soviet Union during the 1990s. About 10 percent of them were scientists; many more were highly educated in other fields. Since their arrival the number of Israeli orchestras has climbed from four to eleven. Just as Russians poured into Israel, so did foreign investment, rising tenfold between 1992 and 1997. Check the phone listings in Israel and you will find research centers for Mitsubishi, IBM, Intel, Motorola and even Siemens, Germany's leading engineering and technology firm.

Back in 1867, Mark Twain toured Palestine and observed: "Of all the lands there are for dismal scenery, I think Palestine must be the prince. The hills are barren, they are dull of color. . . . The valleys are unsightly deserts fringed with a feeble vegetation that has an expression about it of being sorrowful and despondent. It is a hopeless, dreary, heart-broken land."[17]

One hundred years later, visitors to Israel marveled at the grapefruit groves and olive trees that sprang from the desert, along with the Jaffa oranges that delight grocery shoppers from Tel Aviv to London. Today's visitors to Israel don't just stop at the verdant crops. They look agape at the scientific discoveries spawned by a country whose map is studded with tech incubators every few miles and a ratio of 135 engineers for every 10,000 people. Now, Israel is not an utterly free market economy, and its economy is hobbled by high taxes, regulations and international strife and terrorism. Nonetheless, Israel proudly shows that adding intelligent and skilled workers amplifies a country's prospects for prosperity.

Unlike Israel, which has sometimes struggled to handle the deluge of eight hundred thousand Russian refugees who only knew communism, Canada puts out a simple welcome mat inviting skilled workers. Go to the government's Web site and you can read the plain and wise message: "Canada welcomes skilled worker immigrants, and we hope that this Web site will provide you with helpful information about living and working in the various provinces and regions." To top it off, the government site assures you that "applying to come to Canada as a Skilled Worker is not difficult."[18] The U.S. government also has a Web site, of course, but rather than a welcome mat, it is a step into quicksand. During the 1990s new immigrants to Canada accounted for more than 30 percent of the job growth among computer engineers, systems analysts and computer programmers. Unlike the United States, Canada realizes it is competing in a global race for brainpower and skills. In a report called "Stepping Up," a Canadian panel of experts called for even stronger efforts to recruit foreign talent: "Immigrants turned the Canadian West into a breadbox for the world. They fuelled Canada's postwar economic boom, and today they are an important source of higher-order skills for the knowledge-based economy. As a skills channel, immigration offers significant economic advantages to Canada. . . . We must recognize, however, that Canada competes with other nations for skilled immigrants, particularly the United States, Australia, countries of the European Union, and Israel."[19] At least Canada knows it's in a race. The United States looks more like a bumbling bystander who could be run over.

What to Do?

Is Canada a harsh place? Well, in some parts the temperature gets a tad chilly, and only the elk have enough padding to go out in the tundra. But generally, Canada and the Canadian people are described as relatively generous and, if I may say so, more politically liberal than Americans. Canada's (as well as Australia's) immigration system rewards points for education and skills. Instead of exalting blood ties, Canada exalts brains. Why? Not because of snobbery—the landed gentry snobs stayed in England, never bothering to cross the treacherous Atlantic! Canada's immigration program exalts brains because Canada cares a great deal about its future.

First, the United States should take down the altar called family reunification, which accounts for the overwhelming number of legal immigrants. It has led to: chain migrations, an older immigrant population, more burdens on the welfare state and highly concentrated enclaves of immigrants from the same country. As families file in like an endless string of paper dolls, the United States ends up with less diversity and more ghettoized neighborhoods where people do not ever need to learn English.

Second, we should award points for education, work experience, youth (Canada awards the most points for those between the ages of twenty-one and forty-nine) and language proficiency. The United States could accommodate about one million educated people annually, and even more so in the baby boom retirement years after 2010. To alleviate worries about job displacement, during recession years we can temporarily cut back the number of entrants by 10 percent for each one point rise in the unemployment rate.

Although I want to dismantle the reunification altar, I would still offer some points for family relationships in the United States. Family relations help newcomers adapt to a new home but that factor should no longer dominate. Finally, for those who cannot demonstrate educational achievement, possibly because of the poverty or the discriminatory policies of their home countries, I would offer an IQ test. Now, critics might cringe at early-twentieth-century abuses that kept out Jews, Poles and Russians (whose progeny went on to win Nobel prizes!) because of faulty intelligence tests. Nonetheless, for many deprived people in the world an IQ test is a more objective measure. In despotic societies the unintelligent brother of the ruler can claim a Ph.D. In Romania, the wife of the terrifying Nicolae Ceausescu claimed to be a brilliant Ph.D. chemist. After their fall, her teachers displayed the truth: she had dropped out of school after failing everything but needlework, singing and gymnastics. Put to an IQ test the servant who cleaned her bathroom might have proved smarter. IQ testing has progressed since 1900 and can be conducted without language bias. For those who worry that IQ scores will unfairly favor, say, Chinese or Nepalese, we should limit the entrants from any country to, say, 10 percent; from any continent to 35 percent. We want the most talented Asians, Africans, Europeans, South Americans and Australians to come aboard. And if we can persuade some Canadians to head south, that would be fine, too. A ripe place to begin with is the thousands of foreign graduate and postgraduate students.

By elevating intelligence and skills, I'm not suggesting we turn into a nation only of brainiacs who tell jokes in esperanto at Mensa meetings. But human capital does count. And we should have put welcome mats, not barbed wire, in front of the likes of Intel's Andy Grove and Linus Torvalds, developer of Linux. Consider Arnold Schwarzenegger. Back in Austria, if you measured his brain and his motivation, rather than his biceps, he still looked like a good candidate to help the United States. Considering the billion dollars in film revenues he attracted to the United States and his heroic efforts to tackle bankrupt California, it's a good thing that Mr. Universe landed here.

Diversity can work for America when there's some sense behind it. Hip, trendy centers of innovation tend to have diverse populations, with piquant restaurants and vibrant theater and music. If we do not change our current policies, those hip, trendy, wildly productive centers of life will pop up—but outside our borders, where joyous young workers will sing, dance and toast the cool jobs they got from America's outsourcing.

THREE

Education

How the United States Turns Off Students and Turns Over Jobs to Foreigners

During the 1950s and early 1960s, teen movies and songs dominated the world. Kids in Paris wanted to be Frankie Avalon, spreading a beach blanket next to Annette Funicello. Kids in Düsseldorf rocked to the Beach Boys 1963 hit, "Be True to Your School," though I don't know what they made of the lyrics: "My girl will be working on her pom-poms now/And she'll be yelling tonight/So be true to your school . . ." Why was this scene just as exciting to non-Americans as to those who attended Beverly Hills High? An unbelievably simple reason: only the United States had high schools! No wonder our kids were the princes and princesses of the world. Not only that, but in 1955 Disneyland opened up, which promised every American girl that she could wear Cinderella's crown. We had the broadest education system and the strongest economy. Over time, though, the commanding lead in education has evaporated and even reversed.

An old cliché proclaims "I'd rather be lucky than good." Happily, during most of the twentieth century, the United States was both. We had the finest education and economic system in the world. Meanwhile, the rest of the world had lousy systems except for the elites. The post–World War II years looked golden for American businesses. During the Eisenhower years, U.S. automobile and manufacturing firms flattened competitors in Europe and Japan. Why did they succeed so mightily? Because Generals Patton and MacArthur had flattened their factories. When I served in the White House in the early 1990s, doom and gloomers were always harping that we had lost our lead and that blue-collar wages were not holding up compared with the gains of the 1950s and 1960s. Well, it's no great trick to look impressive when the rest of the industrialized world is rolling in rubble. American unions could win huge wage gains without always delivering higher productivity. As the decades wore on, though, international competition picked up and now Americans must fight for every job, every slice of market share and every dime of wage gain.

The education race has also intensified. We are no longer the only country that sends young people to school, even if they have empty wallets. And our education quality is slipping. Thirty years ago, the Gallup Organization reported that nearly 60 percent of Americans had a great deal of confidence in public schools. That score steadily dropped to 36 percent in 1999. Today our schools are like a rusty Ford Pinto from the 1970s: underpowered, underperforming and under threat from nations that are pumping out millions of sleek, smart students. In this chapter we'll spell out the history, the problems and the reforms that can fix our Ford Pinto schools.

Those who block reform dismiss the school crisis and suggest we just tinker with the status quo. They urge more money without offering any proof that it will help, as if adding a zero to a budget will automatically add a number to a meager SAT score. That's the wishful thinking of a gambler, better suited for a Vegas casino than for a school administrator. The United States

may get lucky, of course, and maintain our economic edge even
if we do nothing. But we should not rest our children's future on
a roll of the dice.

First, Some Little History

Okay, let's say you just bought a new digital camera and can't figure out how to take pictures, or download them onto your computer, or watch them on your television. As they asked in
Ghostbusters, "Who you gonna call?" You can choose one of
three "lifelines": a dentist from Cleveland, an elementary school-
teacher from Newark or a college exchange student from India.
Very few would bother to call the teacher. If I gave a quiz in
the 1920s (not about digital devices, of course), you would call the
teacher first. Why? Public schoolteachers used to be among the
smartest, most talented people in the country. In more recent
decades, though, they have slipped further and further beyond
other professions, which we'll discuss in detail later.[1]

You can place any number of labels on the twentieth century,
focusing on world wars, *pax Americana,* or the century when
rock 'n' roll rolled over Beethoven. From an economic point
of view, it was the century when brains trampled brawn, when
farmers left their fields to learn chemistry, when riveters told
their sons to put down their tools and take up optometry. In short,
blue collars faded to white, and incomes rose higher and higher.
By the end of the century, almost every task required literacy. In
the 1960s schools channeled less literate kids into vocational
courses, where they could learn to fix a carburetor. By the 1980s,
fuel injectors replaced carburetors and auto mechanics needed to
understand computer diagnostics.

This transformation ultimately took place across the world as workers moved up the escalator of skills. But, happily for the United States, Americans figured it out first while others lagged for decades. At the beginning of the century, Massachusetts' first commissioner of labor declared that the two assets of Massachusetts were "its climate and its skilled labor." Though a terrible meteorologist, he turned out to be a labor visionary. From 1910 to 1940 the "high school movement" generated skyrocketing graduation rates, from just 10 percent to more than half of American eighteen-year-olds. Though New England originally led the race to the schoolhouse, many regions of the North, Midwest and West surpassed New England, with graduation rates exceeding 50 percent in 1930.[2] In movies about World War II it was still fashionable to show a platoon comprised of men plucked from throughout the fifty states: the wisecracking kid from the Bronx, the naïve farm boy from Kansas, the grits-loving fella from Alabama, et cetera. In reality, by World War II most of the boys would have earned high school diplomas and had far more education than a platoon plucked from the Black Forest of Germany, the piazzas of Italy, or the rice paddies of the Orient.

Instead of schools, Europe (which often ignored the girls' education) pushed boys into apprenticeships, where they learned increasingly obsolete trades. The old world focused general education on its most privileged sons. As late as the mid-1950s, Sweden was the only major European country to send more than 20 percent of its teenagers to schools (compared with 80 percent in the United States). Even though the twentieth century burst with ingenuity and technology, demanding scientists and managers, European boys often whittled away with their fathers' prized tool set. I do not mean to belittle carpentry and masonry. But I do mean to argue that the U.S. educational system gave our young people the intellectual tools to best handle and exploit a century that developed the automobile, airplane and personal computer.

The free enterprise system, of course, induced Americans to put down their fathers' tools and pick up new skills. Those who learned modern skills got paid for it. According to one historical study, if a teenager in 1915 stayed for one additional year of high school, he could fetch 12 percent more money when he looked for work.[3] A fluid labor market encouraged kids to stay in school. They did not need public service announcements on public television.

Why did American schools succeed? While Europe exalted central control, which empowered aristocrats and bureaucrats to dole out funds from the parlors of state capitals, America grew its schools from the ground up like a healthy bumper crop. Tens of thousands of independent school districts raised money from parents and hired principals, who then hired (and, if necessary, fired) teachers without union approval. Citizens willingly paid taxes because they saw the results in their communities; they did not have to wait for Washington bureaucrats to give speeches and convince them that their kids knew an adverb from an aardvark. Parents could tell that the schools worked because they could see their sons and daughters commanding higher wages when they graduated. Here is a key point, seldom made and almost never acknowledged by today's education establishment: in the early decades of the twentieth century, local school districts competed with one another to attract families to their community. Outside of the cities, few people complained of overcrowding and traffic congestion. Rather than repelling people and businesses, they invited them to relocate. Good schools provided a tasty carrot for communities to dangle in front of people looking to relocate.

Competition is not a newfangled idea of today's school choice crowd. Competition helped generate the successes American schools enjoyed from 1900 to the 1960s.

Two things have happened since the early 1960s, though, to dull our edge over the rest of the world. First, our trading partners abroad watched those high school movies and figured out that our huge head start made us richer. Second, we lost our edge because our school quality began to crumble. To avoid admitting this second point, teachers and administrators turned from enhancing skills to enhancing self-esteem. It has worked beautifully. Now our kids have high self-esteem but low test scores. American schools have not made our kids dumb. They've made them delusional.

Does It Matter?

Who cares if students are deluded and score badly on tests? It's common to hear people say that they can depend on their own kids if they ever need help, financial or otherwise. First, the statistics on intergenerational help are not encouraging. Children rarely give money to their parents, and almost one-quarter of the elderly do not have children anyway. My wife and I joke that at the first sign of drool, our kids will stick us in a home. That's why I won't risk eating a ripe peach in front of them. Second, most Americans do not depend on their own kids; they depend on someone else's kids—to provide for their pension, Social Security, health care, meals on wheels, police protection, et cetera. There's a macro and a micro side to this. On the macro side, educated children drive an economy higher, boosting productivity and gross domestic product. On the micro side, an educated person earns higher pay and delivers bigger returns for his employer.

Simply put, America would probably not be as rich today if the high school movement had not taken off a hundred years ago, supercharging the brainpower available for the economy. We often talk of oil, gas and other natural resources that generate horsepower in engines, but brainwaves are also natural resources. Just as spark plugs help ignite combustion in an engine, schools ignited the brainpower that sent the U.S. economy charging ahead, through inventions, innovations and smarter work. Economists, who place brainpower in the category of "labor quality," estimate that a highly educated labor force added between 10 percent to 16 percent of the economic growth over the past forty years.[4] That proportion and our overall GDP (gross domestic product) would have been even higher if the education system had been more robust. Even so, such statistics probably underestimate the value of education. Smarter workers can handle more sophisticated equipment, which inspires firms to develop better tools, driving productivity even higher. UPS drivers are often known for their studly physiques and brown shorts. I'm more impressed with their knowledge of the wireless handheld tracking computers. Smarter drivers with smarter tools make truck delivery faster, safer and more reliable.

Quality over Quantity

"All right, Buchholz, if we are graduating more high school and college kids than ever, why are you complaining?" It's easy to get tripped up by looking merely at the years of schooling instead of at the quality of the schooling and the quality of the teachers.

Schools are not commodities, piles of indistinguishable beans in the back of a kitchen pantry. When we try to figure out how education affects the economy, we get much stronger results when we look at a child's test scores rather than merely the time he spent sitting in a classroom. An analysis of math and science scores across eighty countries showed that higher test scores (a one standard deviation improvement) would push up annual GDP growth by 1 percent.[5] Don't sneeze at 1 percent! An additional 1 percent is enough to spur almost one million new jobs each year and lift incomes by about 65 percent in the next fifty years.

Compared with the rest of the world we do a great job of keeping kids in chairs; a lousy job at instilling knowledge into their brains. If it was a race merely to toughen posteriors, we would be ahead of our trade competitors. The U.S. population averages 12.2 years of school, compared with about 10 years for other advanced and transitional nations. But when we ask our highly experienced student to add, subtract, multiply or divide, they show up at the middle to lower range.[6] More distressing, the longer our kids stay in school, the further they slip behind their peers abroad. Our nine-year-olds do fine, our thirteen-year-olds do middling and our seventeen-year-olds seem to know a whole lot less than most, including Slovenian teens, who obviously have far fewer resources. They avoid the very bottom by squeezing past such troubled places as South Africa and Cyprus. In international comparisons, American students look like the hapless, oft-parodied Jamaican bobsled team. The Brookings Institution estimates that one-fourth of high school seniors, or seven hundred thousand students, do not have the basic skills needed for meaningful work or higher education.[7] Our children are not starting off stupid. IQ scores of five-year-olds have been fairly constant since World War II and are higher than they were in 1900. As each school year goes by, however, you can almost hear those points clicking to the "off" position. By senior year their brains are like eight-cylinder engines limping into the homestretch with a few pinging cylinders left to function.

The lost opportunity shows up in the individual, pocketbook analysis, too. What would happen to American students if they scored one standard deviation higher, in the neighborhood of Czech or Chinese kids? Males would earn almost 19 percent more and females almost 26 percent more. What's this worth to their wallet? Almost $150,000![8] No employer wants to pay for the experience of a worker's gluteus maximus. Only fashion models can make legitimate careers out of shapely posteriors. To earn a middle-class income, you need three kinds of skills: first, hard skills in math, reading and problem solving; second, soft skills, such as the ability to make effective oral and written presentations; third, the ability to use computers to carry out tasks.[9]

With such huge returns, why not just throw more money into the schools? Individual students will grow richer and the U.S. economy will grow bigger. Great investment, no? In fact, we have been throwing more money at schools, but with little to show for it. Inflation-adjusted spending has climbed about 3 percent per student per year for the last century, roughly doubling in the past thirty years.[10] In the last ten years, federal spending alone has doubled. Though stories of overcrowded classrooms often crowd out other newspaper headlines, the student/teacher ratio has actually dropped from about twenty-two to sixteen pupils per teacher. Yet children from around the world trample on our test scores. Immigrants who show up on our shores from countries with high test scores earn more money, because their employers can see the brainpower at work. Something is wrong that won't be solved by adding a few numbers to the budget.

By focusing this chapter on education, I am not claiming that education is the only thing that matters. The Russian Federation has higher test scores, but a far less stable legal, property and overall economic system. Nonetheless, the task here is to show where our society's lapses injure our economy, inviting employers to move jobs to some distant land.

Declining Teacher Quality

I have a confession to make. I like teachers. My mother was a public school teacher, and so was my mother-in-law, as well as many aunts and uncles. If I sound too hard-hearted toward teachers, I will have no place to go for Thanksgiving. Nonetheless, we cannot ignore a basic fact: teachers used to be smarter, especially relative to other workers in the United States. The national No Child Left Behind program should be focused more on teachers, because we need to leave many of them behind in order for the kids to go forward. Teachers used to be among the best educated in society. Teachers born around 1900 averaged about six or seven more years of schooling than nonteachers, but by mid-century their advantage dropped to just two or three years. Compared with other white-collar professionals the figures look even worse. Over time more and more professionals have added post-college to their education; but teachers have dropped out of post-college work. In recent years the plunge has been more dramatic. The proportion of teachers with a master's degree in their subject area plummeted from 17 percent to just 5 percent between 1982 and 2000. A UCLA researcher discovered that 50 percent of the teachers born in the early 1940s scored above the eightieth percentile on the Armed Forces Qualifying Test, but by the early

1960s, only 10 percent scored so highly.[11] Clearly, schools are not hiring the same superstars they hired in years past.

Mystery Solved

What happened? School administrators did not suddenly decide to boycott talented, brainy people. I submit that until the 1960s, schools were heavily subsidized, which gave them and the children a tremendous advantage. The subsidy is now long gone. What kind of subsidy has vanished? We know that federal spending has continued to rise, along with state and local spending. Was it a secret subsidy from the CIA or its predecessor, the OSS? No. In fact, the subsidy was not money. The mysterious subsidy was . . . women. Quite simply, smart women were kept out of other white-collar professions, either by law, custom or societal sneer. The schools benefited because there were few other places for a brainy woman to go. Sure, you could point to the exceptional female doctor or accountant, but the teaching profession could claim almost half of the college-educated women in the 1930s. By the 1970s, only about 10 percent chose the classroom. Today Harvard Law School's graduating class is more than 50 percent women. Fifty years ago a huge proportion of those women would have worked in the classroom, not the courtroom. The same dynamic applies to Howard Law School and the Hershey Medical School. Critics of school choice ask "Why do we need radical reform when public schools used to work just fine?" The answer is this: "Public schools used to perform because women were discouraged from working outside a schoolhouse. Do you want to lock them up again?" Because this subsidy will never return, we need massive reform to fix our schools and equip our children for the competition ahead.

Instead of attracting the most talented people to the front of the classroom, the teaching profession has invented all sorts of dubious credentials to give them the appearance of brainpower. Instead of earning college degrees in reading, writing, 'rithmetic or science, teachers have studied, well, how to teach. But what do they know? That's like giving a blind man a steering wheel and then lecturing him on how to turn left or right. He will easily master the feat of turning the wheel, but what does he know about the road? The speed? The pedestrians in his way? Driving becomes merely a form of aerobic exercise rather than a safe way to transport oneself. Less than 40 percent of teachers have a degree in *any* academic field. Teaching scholar Diane Ravitch says that 120th Street, which separates Columbia's Teachers College from the rest of the university, is known as the "widest street in the world."[12] How many kids drown because their teachers do not cross the street? During his retirement renowned physicist Edward Teller wanted to teach physics at a local high school in California. He was rejected. Not because of his age or controversial politics, but because he lacked the official teaching credential. And so the father of the hydrogen bomb found a Hebrew high school where he could share with students his brilliance and his personal conversation with titans like Einstein and Fermi. The legendary labor leader Albert Shanker said that a love of teaching is not enough: saying that all a good teacher needs is a love of teaching is like saying all a good surgeon needs is a love of cutting. Love and charm are not sufficient. Would you let a charismatic teacher who did not understand surgery teach brain surgery? Then why let an ignorant high school teacher inflict his views on mathematics?

The teaching colleges have also done some damage along the way. In the 1920s, reading researchers told teachers to keep the kids quiet. Not to instill discipline, but because researchers asserted that kids should read "with their eyes, not their ears." Reading aloud would hurt them. Around World War II they took the muzzles off the kids, but then the researchers told the kids to ignore phonics and instead focus on "whole words," which worked great for words like "I" and "A." Only in recent years has the National Institute of Child Health settled the debate, suggesting that teachers bring back phonics and instead put a muzzle on those who believe only in the "whole word" approach.

Union Dos and Don'ts

Unions have not helped the classroom situation, though their influence is far less than the subsidy mystery we solved above. Teachers' unions, like most unions, love credentialism. It keeps down the supply of teachers and raises wages. Unions take power away from the principals and the school boards, making it nearly impossible to fire a tenured teacher, absent the most outrageous acts. Drinking on the job is generally not sufficient; she has to finish the bottle, smash it on the desk and then hit a kid with it. Caroline Hoxby has argued that the unions have been responsible for the dramatic decline in class sizes over the years, even though research does not prove that class size matters very much. Teachers, understandably, prefer smaller classes. They are easier to supervise and more pleasant to work with. I certainly do not blame teachers for seeking smaller classes. More teachers, higher spending and smaller pupil/student ratios match the unions' wish list. Sure enough, we have seen these exact trends over the past thirty years. Meanwhile, the National Education Association and the American Federation of Teachers have seen their market share rise from about 14 percent of districts to more than 70 percent. I would pound the table harder and louder except for one point: the trends in teacher quality, classroom size and per pupil spending were launched long before the unions grabbed their stranglehold on school districts. That is why my suggested reforms are more dramatic than just trying to dilute union power.

Revenge of the Parents

The old song lyric "Don't know much about history, don't know much biology" came in the 1950s but seems more pertinent now. Yet Americans are not stupid, even if they attended mediocre schools. The comic writer Fran Lebowitz said that teenagers should take comfort knowing that in real life there is no such thing as algebra. The truth is, even if Americans cannot solve algebraic equations, they have somehow figured out that better education equals better wages. That's why parents began rebelling a number of years ago. Like the Howard Beale character from the ingenious 1976 movie *Network,* parents have been yelling "We're mad as hell, and we're not going to take it anymore." Well, not literally, of course, but instead of thrusting open windows they have thrust open choices for their children: charter schools, home schools and school choice programs. These are usually the last steps. The first steps are protests to boards of education, hours of volunteering to supplement the teachers and parental networks of homework helpers. It's not easy for parents to take action, of course. Even when they are happy with the schools, most parents feel overwhelmed in their roles. How do they stretch the paychecks to pay for clothes and camp? How do they deal with those hormonal surges that turn their teens into terrors—for thirty minutes, only to reverse and drag them back to sweetness? When will they find the time to figure out their taxes?

The economist Albert O. Hirschman wrote a slim but profound book in 1970 called *Exit, Voice, and Loyalty: Responses to Decline in Firms, Organizations, and States.* He explained how dissatisfied people, whether voters, shoppers or neighbors, prefer to respond through their voice. They complain, they write letters, they meet with decision makers, et cetera. The other option is to pack your bags and take your business elsewhere. Since human beings often have feelings of loyalty, we tend to resist the "exit" strategy. Exit, voice and loyalty show up in the feelings of parents every day. I have many friends in the Washington, D.C., area with children in private schools who feel guilty because they wish they could support the failing public schools. Though loyalty pushes them toward the schools, they do not want to injure their children's prospects by subjecting them to one of the worst educational systems in the country—or on earth, if you consider the international scoring comparisons. We sent one one of my daughters to a highly competitive private school in D.C., but enrolled her in a neighborhood public school when we moved to California. We are not entirely satisfied with the public school, but we are using voice, because the situation is not quite so dire as in D.C. (In fact, D.C.'s school misery seemed so hopeless that Congress finally launched a limited school voucher program allowing about 3 percent of the pupils to opt out of the public schools.)

I'm afraid that most liberals and most bureaucrats believe that Americans are too stupid to exercise either voice or exit. Nonetheless, in every other sphere of our lives we have become a nation of shoppers, a nation of choosers. Most American families can choose from one hundred brands of cereals, one hundred chan-

nels of cable television but just one school. Every fall, hundreds
of thousands of mothers and fathers crisscross the country with
their teenagers checking out college options, inspecting academic offerings, sampling salad bars at the cafeteria and looking
for mildew in dormitory showers. Your local bookstore has a
whole shelf devoted to consumer guides for colleges (and, of
course, automobiles and appliances), and the Internet offers millions of commentaries. Kids who score well on PSATs, or kicking footballs or playing the cello find their mailboxes stuffed
with college brochures.

Considering the scrutiny and the competition, we should not
be surprised that most of the world envies American colleges.
Foreign students beg, borrow and inveigle to attend U.S. colleges
because our colleges are still known for their superior academics
(not to mention sports, theater and coed dancing). How often do
students from Europe and Asia try to finagle their way into an
American public junior high or high school? Seldom, except perhaps to pick up tips on how teens are spiking their hair or pierc-
ing their belly buttons. Do liberals really believe that there is no
connection between competition and outcomes?

Exit: From Fringe to Mainstream

Two of the increasingly popular exit routes are charter schools
and home schooling. What are charter schools? They are public
schools of choice, often exempt from centralized bureaucratic
regulations and usually aimed at a particular mission; for example, arts, science, or foreign language education. Forty-two states
have passed charter school laws, and about seven hundred thousand children attend roughly three thousand charter schools.

Some of the charter schools are simply converted from an existing school with existing faculty; others start fresh. So far the results on charter schools suggest cautious optimism, with test scores somewhat better than conventional public schools. Most interesting, though, is evidence that charter schools run by private education management organizations (EMOs) achieve twice the improvement as charter schools run by non-EMO administrators. Private management skills appear to help, as does breaking almost completely away from the union and bureaucratic choke hold of the central administrators.[13]

Home schooling has also taken off in recent years, with more than thirty states approving the option. Thirty years ago home schooling sounded like an idea from the communes at Berkeley. Then in the 1980s, religious Christian families began to opt out of the public schools, citing worries about drugs, sex and inferior academic skills. I remember when my nonreligious neighbors planned to home school their two children. The mother called a home-schooling support group and asked another mother what kind of math curriculum to use. The woman answered: "I listen and Jesus tells me."

Over the past fifteen years, though, home schooling has reached mainstream, nonideological, religious and agnostic families who have expressed their doubts about public schools. About 3 percent of school-age children now learn at home, and the home schooling population is growing at a quick pace. Reported SAT scores appear to exceed national averages, though it's extremely difficult to compare home schools since every family school is unique. Clearly parents who home school their children have de facto demonstrated an extraordinary devotion to their children's education. They are not loners in a log cabin. They invite other families for recitals, ballgames, and museum visits. When my wife worked at the Kennedy Center for the Performing Arts she noted how home-schooling parents were almost always the first to request student tickets for educational performances. Public schools—burdened by bureaucracy and budget debates—were often last. The more important point, though, is to realize how many parents of all ideological stripes have exited from a failed system.

You can see another kind of voice/exit just by driving around suburbia. David Brooks has noticed that you know you are in a rural community when you see churches, but you are in suburbia when you see lots of Thai restaurants. Next to those Thai restaurants are storefront private businesses offering educational supplements. Two miles from my house is a strip mall offering the following storefronts, along with the typical fabric, furniture and clothing: schools for Spanish and French; ballet; karate; exercise; theater; a teaching supplies store; and two academic tutoring businesses! Once the kids have exhausted themselves and are ready to collapse, there's a Blockbuster video, too. Parents are looking, choosing, spending and not trusting the schools as much as they used to. Parents are so deeply involved and doing so much for their children, I'm sure there are some Little Leagues where after a kid hits the ball, the parents drive him to first base.

What Do We Do?

President Bush's No Child Left Behind Act requires school districts to offer choices, including charter schools, when schools fail to meet their performance goals. Last year 4,800 schools admitted failing, leaving about 2.5 million students even further behind. My point affects more than those 2.5 million: Most of the students attending acceptable schools are receiving unacceptable educations by worldwide standards. Where do congressmen send their children? While just 10 percent of American students attend private school, more than 40 percent of congressmen entrust their kids to private schools, including 46 percent of the Hispanic Caucus and 29 percent of the Black Caucus.[14] They know that most of our children successfully graduating from competent public schools struggle when matched with a student equipped with a high school degree from Korea, Slovenia or Slovakia.

To many people who like to tinker rather than take charge, public charter schools sound like a nice antidote to our ills. It would be great if public charter schools could do the trick and bring back the superior teachers and, more important, superior achievements of American students. But I'm afraid they offer a greatly diluted version of the serious reform needed: true competition. More than one-fifth of D.C. students attend a charter school, and despite the fifteen-thousand-dollar bill that taxpayers fork over for each student, the results are meager. School principals and teachers feel too insulated from competition to respond in dramatic ways. Insulation is great for an attic or for an electrical wire—but it's an appalling thing for a school system. Competition works. And more competition motivates new and existing schools to teach better and demand more from principals, teachers and students. True competition must offer not just carrots but unfortunately a bit of the stick. We have become so focused on coddling and building self-esteem that we have extended it not just to toddlers, not just to fourth graders, but even to the bureaucrats. We have been so tenderhearted that we have been too tenderfooted in walking the path to school reform. Frederick Hess of the American Enterprise Institute has pointed out that if a public school loses kids to a charter school, the principal's job gets easier: fewer kids and probably a spare classroom opens up! If he attracts more students, he's got a bigger burden and must "squeeze students into the last available classroom, add two trailers out back . . . and crowd the school's cafeteria and corridors."[15] Can anyone defend a system that rewards you more for failing and punishes you for becoming more attractive? It's like *Extreme Makeover* in reverse: Ditch the Jennifer Aniston hair and show up like Phyllis Diller.

We cannot expect to build a better system unless we build in tasty carrots and a few stinging sticks. Now this violates our national obsession with feeling good about ourselves. The self-esteem problem goes even beyond elementary schools. A friend who is a professor at Harvard Law School told me that he sees in the classroom the damage of twenty years of self-esteem training. Future lawyers who must be patted on the back and assured that their answers are always right. That's like teaching Dobermans to respond to robbers by begging instead of biting.

We cannot get enough competition without unleashing free enterprise "animal spirits," to borrow John Maynard Keynes's phrase. It has been nearly fifty years since Milton Friedman (Keynes's biggest intellectual rival, though Keynes passed away before Friedman became prominent[16]) proposed scholarships or vouchers with which parents could choose public schools or private schools. But Friedman, despite his breathtaking originality, did not come up with the idea first: 114 years before Friedman's proposal, the state of Vermont launched vouchers, which allow parents across ninety towns to choose schools including private ones. Neighboring Maine has somewhat less experience, having run a successful program only since 1874. In Western Europe, the two highest ranking school systems, the Netherlands and

Belgium, devote the majority of their funds to private institutions.

Opponents worry that school choice rips apart the community fabric by skimming off the best and the brightest from public schools. Here's the clearest way to look at the situation: rich people already have school choice; they can exit for private school anyway. We need school choice so that those middle- and lower income families have freedom of expression: voice and exit. A captive audience does not feel like a happy community. In Jean-Paul Sartre's existentialist play *No Exit,* he describes hell as "other people." That's how people feel when they are stuck in a theater—or a school—with all the exits blocked. That is why private-school teachers, who typically earn less than public schoolteachers, feel happier and more appreciated. They are not guard dogs; they are guides.

When you speak with parents today, you find that most kids have different circles of friends: from school, from soccer, from band, from the swim team, from Sunday school, from camp, and so forth. Sometimes the circles of friends overlap like in a Venn diagram; sometimes not. School choice does not uproot communities; it gives them a deeper grounding because the children graduating will live in more prosperous communities that actually offer them jobs. We should not compare a school choice system with some idealized fantasy of public schools that faded away some forty years ago when *Leave It to Beaver* left the airwaves.

There is more to educational reform than giving parents a voice and exit. As I have discussed in this chapter, we must refocus teachers so that they actually know something about the subjects they are teaching. I want my younger daughter's kindergarten teacher to be cuddly and fun. But I want my older daughter's algebra teacher to sparkle with intelligence and knowledge. We must admit that it is tougher—and more expensive—to find engaging math and science teachers. So pay them more! This annoys union protocol, but we have to break out of fairy-dust land and face reality. You've probably heard the saying that "Those who do, do. Those who can't, teach. And those who can't teach, teach phys ed." That's unfair, of course, but everyone knows that teaching kickball is easier than teaching calculus. We should also fight the silly credentialism and encourage scientists, engineers and others to enter the classroom. Right now, there is a 40 percent chance that your child's science teacher "don't know much about a science book," lacking even a college minor in the subject. Would you rather have your son taught physics by a Ph.D. from NASA who took an intensive eight-week course on teaching methods or a graduate of a four-year teaching college who tried to avoid the hard sciences?

Denver recently shrugged off pressure from the NEA and adopted a merit pay program that rewards teachers for getting advanced certificates in math and science and grants them big bonuses based on student test scores. Working with the local teachers' union, the school district designed a wide-ranging pay scale, from starting salaries at thirty-three thousand dollars to a maximum of one hundred thousand dollars for master teachers. The assistant superintendent posed a persuasive question: would you rather pay a raise "simply on the basis of seniority, or would you want to direct the money to rewarding teachers who meet objectives?"[17] It's nice to honor our elders, but we should not assume that a few more wrinkles automatically make someone a better teacher.

All over the world tonight, students are writing research papers, learning new languages and figuring out how to unravel a complicated word problem that asks what time a plane will arrive in London if it's traveling 500 miles per hour with a full load of fuel and is showing a two-and-a-half-hour movie. Whose children will learn the new language? Whose children will come up with the right answers? Whose children will be equipped with the critical thinking skills to work through the problems? Are we so foolish and irresponsible that we can believe that those children who fail will be the ones offered the best jobs in this century? Some will get lucky, of course. But America has never depended solely on luck. Lucky and good win every time.

FOUR

The Taxman Cometh and Taketh

How Taxes, Social Security and Medicare Punish U.S. Workers and Send Their Jobs Abroad

They say in the future a typical factory will host three workers: a man, a computer and a dog. The computer will do all the work. The man will feed the dog. And the dog's job? To bite the man if he touches the computer.

Now the outsourcing outcry warns us that even that factory will be somewhere offshore. With the GDP galloping along in 2003 and 2004, economists had been predicting millions of new jobs, if only to count the coins ringing in the cash registers. With competition from outsourcing, though, jobs failed to come along until the spring of 2004, not nearly as soon as in past recoveries. Today the job prospects for a dog may seem better than for a fiber optic Ph.D. in Boise or a call center operator in Bismarck. (Note that shares of Petco Animal Supplies leaped by 100 percent in the middle of 2003.)

Here's a simple question to highlight the problem. If you were a company manager, why would you hire a human being instead of a machine? Humans get sick, they use toilets, they cough. Now it's true that old-fashioned machines used to squirt oil and grease. But today a factory floor looks cleaner than a hospital operating room. And in high-tech chip plants, they wear the same booties and hairnets as they do on *ER*. All they lack is a star like George Clooney or Noah Wyle.

There's more to the argument than hygiene, though. For instance, money. The cost of capital equipment from laptops to lathes has plummeted. Moreover, the cost of leasing and financing new tools has plunged to the lowest levels since, well, before we had laptops and lathes. From 2001 to 2004, Alan Greenspan's generous lending window gave money to the hands of businesses. Don't get me wrong; that was a good thing. At the same time U.S. tax policy has been tilted toward capital, with dividend and capital gains taxes falling to 15 percent. Small businesses could immediately write off a hundred thousand dollars in new equipment while big firms got a special 50 percent bonus write-off. Nice time to be selling gadgets and gears. The stock market noticed and catapulted shares of machinery companies up by about 40 percent in 2003.

And what about people? With all due respect to Barbra Streisand, "people who need people" aren't the luckiest people in the world anymore. An enormous hurdle stands between employers and job applicants in the United States. Let's say an applicant can deliver thirty-five thousand dollars of value for the firm and that she is willing to work for thirty-five thousand dollars. Great match, right? No. On top of the salary, the employer also has to pay a 7.65 percent Social Security and Medicare tax and contribute to workers' compensation and unemployment insurance. And let's not forget health care averaging sixty-six hundred dollars per family, along with the possibility that the employee will draw on the Family Medical Leave Act. All of those costs are going up, not down. So, the happy job applicant who could create thirty-five thousand dollars of value might actually *cost* the firm fifty thousand dollars. Economists call this the wedge, and it's more painful to workers than any wedgie they ever received at summer camp.

When job applicants show up at the door, managers look at them with dread, like a walking bill from a collection agency. President Bush's income tax cuts chipped away at the hurdle, but the imposing hurdle is still growing higher—just when the hurdle for capital has been shrinking to the height of a sidewalk curb. By the time the boss adds the numbers, outsourcing to those eager, well-spoken kids in India seems pretty attractive, too. Can anything be done? Well, we certainly shouldn't dissuade businesses from investing in machines. Supersized productivity gains push up our standard of living.

In this chapter we will take a close look at the wedge and figure out how to alleviate the pain and make American workers more attractive. The aging of America makes the challenge more severe while also adding urgency to the task. We will also see how our corporate tax system sends jobs offshore and suggest how to diminish that wedge as well. We might not be able—or want—to level the playing field between the high-wage United States and the paltry wages payable in India. But right now we have a field that's tilted for reasons having nothing to do with our standard of living. Unless we do something, millions of American jobs may roll off the field, like marbles when a toddler hurls a Chinese checkerboard across the room.

Sticky Labor Markets and the Entitlement Wedge

Economists like fluid markets. I don't mean the market for drinks, though a Scotch has comforted many Wall Street economists when their forecasts have proved screwy. Economists like markets that move smoothly, with lots of buyers and sellers who can move swiftly. Is the American job market fluid? "Sticky" might be a better word. You want to hire someone? Call your human resources office and flip through the loose-leaf notebook of ever-changing regulations and tax deductions. You want to fire someone? Call a lawyer, especially if the person has any noticeable medical, ethnic or age characteristic. A few years ago the National Symphony Orchestra was sued by a Russian-born violinist who was fired for being a bad fiddler. He sued the NSO for discriminatory dismissal, claiming that the associate conductor was German-born and possibly the son of a Nazi father. These days employers are scared to answer the telephone to offer honest assessments of former employees, for fear of a lawsuit.

We'll deal more with the legal hazards in Chapter 6, but for now let's focus on the economic stumbling blocks. Here is a key point not found in most discussions about the wedge: Not only must employers worry about the current tax system, but they must also worry about the potential for massive tax hikes in the future to fund entitlement programs like Social Security and Medicare. These public programs are heading toward bankruptcy just like the private pyramid schemes that have hoodwinked people in the past. So to correctly gauge the wedge we must examine the current plight and the upcoming debacle.

How'd we get into this mess? We've spent seventy years building a pyramid scheme. When Franklin Roosevelt set up the Social Security system, the median age of a retired worker was, well, "dead." It was easy to promise benefits when most people died in their fifties—before they were eligible at sixty-five. A pyramid scheme works as long as you've got an ever bigger supply of drones to lug the bricks and blocks. Pyramids worked fine for the pharaohs until Charlton Heston led the Hebrew slaves through that river. In 1937 Social Security Taxes (Old-Age and Survivors Insurance) took just 2 percent of wages, with a maximum annual tax of $60. Even by 1951, the tax was just 3 percent, with a maximum of $108. Today, workers pay 10.7 percent with a maximum of nearly $10,000. When politicians promise lower taxes, they seldom are willing to attack this huge wedge, which will be growing larger unless we launch revolutionary reform. Already more than 80 percent of families pay more in payroll taxes (including the employer's share) than in income taxes! And those taxes bring in as much revenue to the government as the income tax, more than 40 percent, compared with about 15 percent in 1960.

These figures do not even count the yoke of state and local taxes, but the yoke is cracking certain regions. Philadelphia has paid a heavy price for heavy taxes. The City of Brotherly Love might as well be the City of "Brother, Can You Spare a Dime?" If the job market had stood still, that would have been an improvement. Instead, Philadephia has shed hundreds of thousands of jobs since 1970. The city squeezes an additional 4.46 percent tax from workers' pockets beyond federal and state taxes. And if you live over the Ben Franklin Bridge in New Jersey, not only do you pay a toll to get across but you also pay a 3.88 percent city wage tax. "Stay home!" That's the message. And people sure did, even during the booming 1990s. The Federal Reserve Bank of Philadelphia estimates that a hundred thousand Philadelphians lost their jobs because of the wage tax between 1977 and 1984.[1] It's hard to worry about a crack in the Liberty Bell when the job market is so broken. Finally, in 2003 the city's Tax Reform Commission recommended slicing the wage tax. I hope they act. It's painful to watch a city that celebrates liberty imprisoned by stupid policies.

Just as wage taxes sent Philadelphia firms packing to go to Wilmington, Phoenix and Portland, so can federal taxes send businesses offshore. By ignoring tax competition among countries we have been jeopardizing jobs. As the world economy grows more competitive and managers have to figure out how to preserve thin profit margins, taxes will carry even more weight. Firms that export are the most nimble and the most sensitive to how much money they send to Uncle Sam or Uncle Samurai, as the case may be.[2]

The expanding size of the tax wedge especially punishes young people. Elderly retirees have gotten back almost twice as much from Social Security as they paid in. In contrast, younger workers will fetch just fifty cents for every dollar they send to Washington. For example, a thirty-five-year-old earning an average income will fork over $135,000 more than he will receive in benefits! If he is lucky enough to earn twice the average, he can say good-bye to $274,000.[3] With such a gaping hole in workers' pockets, how can we expect them to save for retirement? Imagine: an average worker needs to squirrel away an extra $135,000 just to stay even. "Squirrel" is the right word because the scenario sounds like a rodent on a treadmill going nowhere.

Cracking Pyramids

The pyramid scheme worked okay for a while. During the 1930s, President Roosevelt heard the wails of old people, many of whom were too feeble to find work during the Great Depression and were almost three times more likely to be poor than the average American. Now their chances of being poor are about the same. Moreover, their chances of owning a home are higher. Today a seventy-five-year-old American is more likely to own his home than a sixty-five-, or fifty-five- or forty-five- or thirty-five-year-old. Older people are happier with their financial situation than other age groups, with just 12 percent expressing dissatisfaction, compared with 30 percent for the rest of the working age population.[4]

But what comes next? The forecast is not good. It reminds me of Woody Allen's line that mankind faces a crossroads: "One path leads to despair and utter hopelessness. The other, to total extinction. Let us pray we have the wisdom to choose correctly." Economists have been crunching numbers to develop generational accounting systems, which basically ask the following question: How much are we ripping off our children and grandchildren by promising retirement and medical services to ourselves? One of the leading analysts, Laurence Kotlikoff, estimates that tax rates will have to rise by nearly 70 percent to pay the bills now accruing.[5]

This staggering conclusion jumps out from the demographic headstand taking place. When the U.S. Congress invented Social Security, the ratio of young to old was about ten to one. Soon after World War II, the suburbs blossomed, bringing gurgling babies, new schools and a seemingly endless supply of future workers to pay for their elders. Now the scene has changed; the channel has been changed. The U.S. population is turning upside down. We have never performed a collective headstand before and the degree of difficulty is treacherously high. Our fastest growing group is our slowest moving, the over-eighty-five-year-olds, a population that will double to eight million by 2030 and more than double again to eighteen million in 2050, making up 5 percent of the population. The coming clash between young and old is not just history repeating itself. The history of every civilization going back to ancient Egypt is sprinkled with clichés about old people's resenting boisterous, vulgar, partying children, and children in return resenting stodgy authority figures. A gray-bearded Moses really did hurl down the tablets on a carousing crowd, didn't he? Was the dance around the golden calf a rave?

This time, though, the generational dynamic is really different. How? First, until the late-twentieth century, the United States had always had many more young people than old people. We were the New World bouncing with newborn babies. Abraham Lincoln presided over ten times as many five- to fourteen-year-olds as people over sixty-five. When my grandparents were kids in the 1920s, they outnumbered their grandparents five to one. Even during the Nixon years (speaking of stodgy authority figures) schoolkids still clung to a two to one advantage. Those were the days. By 2050, senior citizens will turn the tables and outnumber schoolkids two to one. The second reason it's different this time is that old people don't seem nearly so old so soon. Although they may retire earlier than ever before, they want to keep spending. Many of them expect to spend more years enjoying retirement than years they spent working. I've gone on cruise vacations to Alaska and watched thousands of liver-spotted hands waving at the whales. But I've also been jostled while waiting in line to go kayaking.

We already have more golf courses in America than McDonald's. Soon we will have more walkers than strollers. Who will pay for them when for every codger on the golf course there are just two or three young, low-wage tip-dependent caddies sweating so that they can keep up with the retiree's pension, Social Security, health benefits, and so on?

Why does this affect outsourcing? The point is that when a firm decides to hire an American, it is agreeing to take on the awesome burden and frightening uncertainty. Why not go to India, which promises far less and won't face the demographic collapse until fifty years after the United States begins to suffer? Especially in a country with sticky hiring and firing requirements, firms cannot ignore future burdens. The burden might not be so far off, either. The Me Generation of baby boomers will start retiring in just a few years. The boomers themselves helped create the problem. Remember those 1960s placards that warned about the population explosion, and discouraged some parents from bringing children into the cruel world? Between 1970 and 1980, the number of schoolkids actually dropped 14 percent. By lowering the birthrate in the 1960s and 1970s, boomers heaved more economic responsibility onto the shoulders of those children who actually were born. Here's the irony: By having fewer kids and yet promising themselves more benefits, the boomers created the population time bomb—but it's not their children. The boomers are the bomb!

Of course, other industrialized nations are facing similar traps. Japan and Germany, for example, are performing even more dangerous headstands than the United States and governments face stiff resistance when they suggest reform. In Japan, which is aging faster than sushi, the ratio of workers to retirees will reach one to one in 2044. A poll of twentysomethings showed that 81 percent did not trust the national pension system. Not that the system has much credence among middle-aged people, either. Seven of Prime Minister Junichiro Koizumi's cabinet have failed to pay into the pension plan. The opposition party was ready to pounce with indignation—until they discovered their leader had also shirked his duty. To shore up its finances, the government has jacked up premiums 35 percent and slashed pension payments by 15 percent.[6] There is more to come. A society sewn together by the Confucian ethos of seniority is ripping itself apart. The old story about Eskimos' sending their elders out of the igloos to go off and die with dignity doesn't seem so far-fetched after all.

In Germany former chancellor Helmut Kohl caught hell just for suggesting that German workers cut back their annual spa visits, for which the government pays them to loll about in bubbly waters. Only Britain has tackled the pension problem, thanks to the Iron Lady, Mrs. Thatcher, who partially privatized Social Security.

Raw Deal

The United States has been encouraging earlier retirement ever since the Union Army started mailing out Civil War pensions. Further, the entitlement programs discourage people from earning and saving on their own, especially spouses (typically women) and minorities. How so? Let's use an example from the recent book *The Coming Generational Storm*. Take two couples: Bob and Karen and Charlie and Lauren. Bob and Charlie both sell cars and earn about $75,000. Karen "works a grueling night-time shift as a nurse's aide . . . earning $20,000, on which she pays $2,480 (including the employer contribution) in Social Security payroll taxes."[7] Lauren doesn't bother working; she spends her days at the golf course perfecting her putting. Here's the question: Come retirement, how much more will Social Security send to Karen compared with Lauren in appreciation for her $2,480 contribution over forty years? The answer: not a penny. Why? While her spouse Bob is alive, Karen will collect more as a dependent spouse than she'd collect based on her payroll taxes. When Bob dies, she'll collect as a survivor all that Bob would have enjoyed. So dead or alive—whether she liked him or not—Bob's contributions made Karen's totally unnecessary. Meanwhile, Lauren must have a pretty good putt and maybe a hell of a drive as well.

The Social Security squeeze probably cheats blacks and Hispanics, too. For one thing, these groups are overrepresented among young people and underrepresented among boomers. Fewer than 18 percent of boomers are black or Hispanic, but 33 percent of children are. Black men can expect to die seven and a half years sooner than whites, which reduces their chances of collecting on the entitlement promises. A Rand Corporation study found that Social Security forces blacks to fork over between two thousand dollars and twenty-one thousand dollars to whites.[8] All this, when black families have an average net asset value of zero. After all, black families are typically poorer than whites, and poorer people tend to start working earlier in life and die sooner, collecting fewer benefits. With these perverse flows, why should minority generations X, Y and Z have any sympathy toward tax hikes to keep the system going? Social Security was part of the New Deal, but is turning into the raw deal.

For those who think I may be exaggerating the challenge, I urge you to open your mail. The Social Security Administration has probably sent you a letter this year spelling out your earnings record. Here's the warning that came in Commissioner Jo Anne Barnhart's January 2004 letter:

> Unless action is taken soon to strengthen Social Security, in just 15 years we will begin paying more in benefits than we collect in taxes. Without changes, by 2042 the Social Security Trust Fund will be exhausted. By then, the number of Americans 65 or older is expected to have doubled. There won't be enough younger people working to pay all of the benefits owed to those who are retiring. At that point, there will be enough money to pay only about 73 cents for each dollar of scheduled benefits. We will need to resolve these issues soon. . . .

If she sounds panicky, don't you think employers will think twice or thrice about hiring here?

The FUTA Football

In addition to Social Security payroll taxes, the federal government bites off an extra 0.8 percent under the Federal Unemployment Tax Act (FUTA). The bite comes out of the first seven thousand dollars of wages and adds up to seven billion dollars' to ten billion dollars' being wired annually to the IRS for safekeeping. But it's not supposed to be for safekeeping. The federal government is supposed to give the money back to the states to administer and help pay for unemployment insurance programs. Instead, half the money gets dumped into a pseudotrust fund. Here's a valuable lesson: never trust a government trust fund. Even though the trust fund bulges with tens of billions of dollars that Washington won't let go of, Congress has kept in place a "temporary" surtax on FUTA since . . . (drumbeat) . . . 1976! The 0.2 percent surtax was due to expire in 1987, but Congress has voted five times to keep the money rolling in. Every time a congressman holds up his hand to vote yes on its extension, he's probably throwing some constituents out of work by incrementally driving up labor costs.

Although the Bush administration has tried to cut off the temporary surcharge and deflate the FUTA football to about 0.2 percent, the opposition battles fiercely. Who's fighting over the football? Battalions of self-interested civil servants who like the bloated status quo and an incestuous system of money flows between Washington and state capital bureaucrats. New York's Department of Labor sent out an urgent, boldface memo to its public employees entitled "**Call to Action—Save DOL Jobs!!!**" The memo denounced Bush's plan and asked "your help to defeat these proposals to ensure . . . your job security."[9] Funny, I did not think that the Department of Labor's priority should be keeping more people on its payroll. Maybe it'll get lucky and the country will roll into a recession so it'll have even more things to do. The chairperson of the New York Public Employees Federation testified passionately before the House Ways and Means Committee: "The president's proposal is of critical interest to the 53,000 member NYS Public Employees Union," he said in his first sentence. In the second sentence he described the urgent work of his members, including "protecting the public in a myriad of ways such as inspecting the safety of amusement rides and ski lifts."[10] So the stakes are indeed high. The furor and misplaced priorities remind me of the story of the crying bureaucrat at the overstaffed Bureau of Indian Affairs. "Why are you crying?" someone asks. "My Indian died."

The Dangerous Medicare Headstand

If the Social Security payroll system sounds rickety, the Medicare system sounds like a patient in the intensive care unit getting constant transfusions. Now, you may think that because Medicare covers old people employers don't care much about it. But they do for two reasons. First, Medicare's 2.9 percent payroll deduction does contribute to the wedge, which pushes apart employers and prospective employees. Unlike Social Security's tax, which gets capped after the first $87,900 of earnings, you keep paying Medicare up to the very last dollar. Second, even if an employer hires only young people, he must consider that Medicare taxes will be going up in the future, maybe soon. Young people will be forced to pay for their parents, grandparents and even elderly strangers. Just because an employer does not hire elderly strangers does not mean that the employer gets off scot-free from an eventual Medicare blowup. Congress has already jacked up the Medicare tax from its 1960s level, which was just 0.7 percent on the first $6,600 (instead of 2.9 percent on every dollar). It would be nice if the already stiff tax were sufficient to pay the upcoming bills, but the storm clouds are darkening and our instruments seem to be spinning backward as we lose altitude.

The Medicare headstand does not come from government treachery, but rather from good news: we're living longer. Most people didn't worry much about hospital bills in 1900, when most people dropped dead before fifty and barbers performed dental surgery, pulling out infected buck teeth in between a shave and haircut. Medical technology and better diets have pushed life expectancy toward eighty. And today it's not surprising to see a seventy-year-old playing tennis, scuba diving or running his winded grandkids ragged on a basketball court. Nonetheless, bodies eventually give in to infection, disease and gravity. About half of senior citizens do eventually need nursing-home care. The greater our success in extending longevity, the more it costs in the end. The sickest (and generally oldest) 3 percent of our population consumes 40 percent of the health dollars. Even after adjusting for inflation, Americans spend eleven times what they spent on health care prior to World War II.[11]

Just as seniors and baby boomers are living longer, they are also becoming more vain. Advertisements for face-lifts, face peels, tummy tucks, breast implants and butt implants seem to fund every magazine in America named after a city or state, whether San Diego, Chicago or Texas. Botox parties started sprouting up a few years ago, with women (and some men) lining up for injections of poisonous compounds. A friend of mine who works in Hollywood as a casting agent says she cannot find middle-aged actresses who can frown on camera. We're not talking about acting talent to compete with Meryl Streep. Even a frown becomes a lost skill when your facial muscles are paralyzed.

With smooth foreheads and limber muscles from yoga, you might think that older people will keep going to work, especially because physically demanding jobs in the mines or the steel mills have been replaced by desk jobs. If people worked longer and expected government retirement and medical benefits later, perhaps the cratering entitlement programs could be salvaged. No such luck. History shows that the better we feel, the easier the work and the longer we live, the sooner we want to quit and spend our golden years playing. In 1880, three-quarters of those who lived to sixty-four kept working (presumably they couldn't afford to retire). By 1950, this figure dropped to 50 percent, on its way to roughly 20 percent today. Many Americans who retire today are vigorous enough to hold up their gold watch retirement gift and use it as a stopwatch to jog home. In Europe we see similar patterns. In fact, in France only 10 percent of those over sixty-four still work. Why should they? The welfare state entices them to relax by the sea.[12] No wonder surveys show that younger Americans feel a tinge of envy. Fifty-five percent of those under sixty-five think their financial security and their enjoyment of life will improve after hitting sixty-five. An amazing 79 percent even thought their love life would either stay the same or improve![13] The combination of Botox and Viagra must be staggering.

The Problem with Other People's Money

So what's the problem? Sounds like Rip van Winkle would be lucky to fall asleep on the job at forty-five and wake up at sixty-five. The problem comes when senior citizens expect younger people to foot the bill. Already, two-thirds of seniors depend chiefly on Social Security to pay the monthly bills and almost all depend on Medicare to pay for their health. Unfortunately, our health-care system does not give retirees a big enough incentive to watch where the money goes. A Medicare card feels like you are wielding someone else's credit card, literally, the credit card that belongs to other people's children. Economists call this the moral hazard problem. Did you ever rent a car and decide to wash it before returning it? Have you ever been on vacation at a fancy hotel and instead of dipping in the pool, asked the concierge to get you a sponge, a long hose and a bucket? Of course not. In fact, people treat rental cars less gingerly than their own, daring to parallel park in the tightest spots and slamming their foot on the accelerator to launch themselves up the freeway entry ramp. Likewise, if Medicare is paying 80 percent of your bills, you might decide on a whim to drop by the podiatrist's office for a pedicure. Instead of buying a $10 heating pad, you might first spend $250 to talk to an orthopedic surgeon. These dynamics are not found only in Medicare. Employer-paid health insurance can lead to the same waste. Empirical studies show that people shop more carefully when the money comes from their wallets. A Rand Corporation study showed that when people are "free riders" on someone else's policy, they rack up 45 percent more in medical bills. More striking—they don't end up any healthier! Raising out-of-pocket costs by 10 percent would cut medical spending by 6.2 percent. Intensive care patients in Miami spend twice as much as those in Minneapolis but do not come out any healthier. More medical spending does not guarantee better health, any more than expensive, high octane fuels get a car to last longer or burn less of it.[14]

Spending other people's money creates extra demand, drives up prices and drives down job numbers. As health-care costs gallop past a 10 percent annual pace, employers have less incentive to hire more people and a growing incentive to pressure existing workers to log longer hours. How so? A health-care insurance policy is a fixed cost. Faced with a choice of hiring two people to each work thirty hours a week or pressuring one person to work sixty hours, the manager would prefer the latter. That way he does not have to provide a second health-care policy.[15]

America's national sport is shopping. That's our advantage,

just like basketball and baseball in the Olympics. We need to use our well-honed skills to our advantage in order to save young people from the crushing burden of entitlements. And in order to make young people in America more appealing to employers.

What to Do?

After considering the gloomy path ahead, you'll want to throw your favorite chair and your flat panel TV into your SUV and, like *The Beverly Hillbillies* in reverse, drive back to the Ozarks beyond the pale of civilization. And beyond the absurd promises of Social Security and Medicare. Unlike Jed Clampett, you probably won't want to hitch granny to the roof because she'll just bankrupt you with the cost of her blood pressure and arthritis pills. The Social Security mess and the even bigger Medicare mess demand radical reform. While the term "radical" usually conjures up Dead Head followers of Jerry Garcia and Che Guevara, the word comes from the same humble root as "radish"; that is, "root." Even conservatives can be radical when it's necessary to get to the root, just as Ronald Reagan realized the root of the Soviet-U.S. nuclear standoff was a combination of ideological evil and an appeasement mentality that had gripped the U.S. State Department.

How do we get to the root of Social Security? By first admitting that it is ripping off our children and denying young people job opportunities.

We must win over young people who now have no stake in forking over more money. Some clever polls showed that more young people believed in the existence of UFOs than in Social Security's survival. And when asked which they thought would live longer, they chose the soap opera *General Hospital* over Medicare.[16] The solution commonly heard in Washington is unimaginative and unresponsive: turn to young people, and say, "We're going to pinch you harder and raise your payroll taxes." Then turn to boomers and say, "We're going to shave back those promises." Unfortunately, this answer just widens the wedge between prospective employers and employees. It may sound Solomonic, but instead of saving the program, it just shrinks the economy.

Here's what we can do to remember three key principles:

1. Young workers and old people must have a stake in the future
2. Payroll taxes create a wedge and disincentive to hiring
3. Everyone should have "skin in the game"; i.e., not spend someone else's money willy-nilly

The good news, if there is any, is that young people are much more skilled at self-help and doing it yourself than prior generations. We shop at Home Depot, book our own flights online and trade stocks without paying exorbitant fees to middlemen. Young people are more willing to take matters into their own hands than their parents. The very idea that the federal government should be taking their money, purportedly buying U.S. treasuries and then promising a shaky return strikes young people as, well, a science fiction story with a bad ending. Might as well make Ben Affleck president and get over with it.

We should junk the payroll tax and thereby discard the lethal wedge. (In fact, I would favor junking the entire federal income tax and replacing it with a simple sales tax. To avoid extracting too much from poorer families, the government could exempt food and clothing and then refund the first twenty thousand dollars paid by each family.) What about grandma and grandpa already retired? Continue paying them their promised benefits. What about baby boomers ready to retire? Pay them the money that's accrued in their accounts. What about young people? Give them back the money that Social Security has already taken, but require them to regularly deposit funds in a personal retirement account, which can be invested in a combination of privately managed stock or bond funds, depending on their own personal appetite for risk. Furthermore, I would require workers to make regular deposits to an annuity that would, by age sixty-five, ensure that their income did not fall below the poverty zone. Unlike the payroll tax, though, the deposits could come from any number of sources, including, for example, family gifts or a reverse mortgage on a home.

No solution is perfect, of course. But so far our politicians have been foolish enough to think that we can support old people at a level totally disconnected from the state of the general economy. Under the program outlined above, if the economy performs well for the next fifty years, young workers will prosper, both in their incomes and in their investment returns. A weak, collapsing economy cannot afford to pay the bills of pensioners.[17]

Moreover, insisting that workers have some "skin" in the investment world will create a louder voice for smarter monetary and fiscal policy. It will reduce the ability of crooked politicians to fool voters into thinking that big taxes and big spending makes people richer, when all it really does is aggrandize politicians by creating more dependents.

Medicare begs even more urgently for a solution. We must slice and dice the credit card that allows people to shop with other people's money. As I said earlier, we are champion shoppers, but our system treats us like dolts. Here's a two-pronged attack: First, strongly encourage or require young workers to start contributing to a private health-insurance policy that will pay benefits when they retire. The sooner they contribute, the cheaper the policy. The better they take care of themselves, the cheaper the policy. They won't need the government to force them to put down their doughnuts and cigarettes. Such a policy would cost far less than the 2.9 percent chunk that Medicare bites off from every dollar they ever earn.

Second, workers should be strongly encouraged or required to establish tax-free medical savings accounts (MSAs) to cover costs during their working years. Under an MSA, they could buy catastrophic coverage while pouring the savings into a tax-free account that they controlled. A worker could dip into the MSA to pay for routine bills. However, the amount he does not touch would build up tax free into a nice retirement nest egg. Here's the key point: MSAs give people a reason to think twice before spending money willy-nilly on medicine and doctors, because the money does come out of their pocket.

Under this program, do you throw old people out of the hospitals? Of course not. But you erase the melt-down scenario and you alleviate employers' real fears that they will be stuck with America's medical expenses. By unleashing the shopping genius of Americans, you could cut the wedge that drives jobs offshore.

Of course, politicians will be politicians; that is, timid and slow to act. The lesson is to give them less power and less authority over our money. Congressmen are still frightened by the harrowing story of Representative Dan Rostenkowski, who pushed through a catastrophic health-care plan for the elderly and then asked them to help pay for it. The *Chicago Tribune* described the powerful leader being "booed and chased down a Chicago street . . . by a group of senior citizens . . . eventually the six-foot four-inch Rostenkowski cut through a gas station, broke into a sprint and escaped in a car, which minutes earlier had one of its protesters, Leona Kozien, draped over the hood."[18]

Well, if granny is going to jump on your car anyway you might as well, like Jed Clampett, take her with you to escape the vicious tax squeeze to come.

The Corporate Tax Dodge

Let's start with a basic idea. Corporations are not people; when you prick them they do not bleed. So when you tax them, they do not bleed. Who does? Shareholders and employees. Now back in the marijuana-fogged sixties, when left-wingers hated capitalism and wanted to punish shareholders by driving down profits, that might have seemed like an interesting route. But in a country where today half the families own shares, it sounds like a silly idea. I'm reminded again of the great and prophetic film *Network*, in which a Communist Angela Davis-type gets to host a television show. Pretty soon she dumps her Marxist cant and screams something along the lines of: "I want my profits! Look at my ratings!" I'm also reminded that when I bumped into that proletarian filmmaker Michael Moore at the Detroit airport, he was preboarding for his first-class seat.

Corporate taxes also hit employees, of course. Rather than rant about abolishing the corporate income tax, I'd like to focus on the well-publicized, highly denounced issue of U.S. corporations' moving headquarters offshore. Naturally, when top executives pull out their headquarters and anchor offshore, they send pink slips to American employees, whether they are moving to Bermuda, Dublin or Abu Dhabi. Taxes matter. One researcher surveyed executives who had launched eighty different projects in various industries. They were asked which factor was deemed so crucial that they would have abandoned the project without it. Almost 50 percent named taxes as the most important factor.[19] Sure enough, as other countries have cut their corporate tax rates, the United States finds it more difficult to keep corporations here. It was easier in the early 1960s to keep firms home. After all, most of the world was still reeling from the destruction of World War II. In 1960, 90 percent of the world's biggest firms (top twenty) made America their home. Today less than half do. That number could shrink further if we allow corporate taxes to scare them off.

Keep in mind two aspects of the problem: First, the federal corporate tax rate at 35 percent does not look very inviting anymore, especially when state and local governments snatch an additional 5 percent. Our 40 percent effective rate is one-third higher than the Organization of Economic Cooperation and Development average and even higher than France and Germany's! The average rate in the thirty OECD countries has plunged 20 percent since 1997, from about 37 percent to 30 percent.[20] India and the Philippines post rates 10 percent to 20 percent below U.S. rates. And let's not even talk about Ireland's 12.5 percent rate. No wonder dozens of U.S. firms have rechartered themselves as non-U.S. firms. Rather than denouncing their patriotism, politicians should recognize the forces that push them offshore. The Reagan revolution swept much of the world late in the 1990s. But that revolution continues, and thereby continues to make the globe a highly competitive place. Great for consumers, but challenging for those who like tax collectors.

Second, the United States burdens its firms with a worldwide tax system that says: "We will seek you out and tax you for any dollar, pound, euro, yen, yuan or rand you earn anyplace in the world. And we don't care if you made the profit on a computer you built in China and sold in Norway. We don't care if no American on American soil ever touched the darn thing." This would not be so bad, but the firms already have to pay profit taxes to the country in which they sold the goods.

Most other major countries take a territorial approach. A Dutch company that sells the goods in Norway pays only the Norwegian tax. The Dutch tax authorities are not so avaricious and therefore do not have to be so snoopy. This gives Dutch firms a big incentive to go after foreign sales, but no incentive to drag their headquarters offshore.

Even Representative Charles Rangel, the senior Democrat on the Ways and Means Committee, has admitted the idiocy of current policy: "It is no longer a question of whether the U.S. tax code encourages the export of American jobs. We now know it does."[21]

But wait; the idiocy gets worse: According to the Joint Committee on Taxation, Congress's nonpartisan scorekeeper, the twisted rules do not even raise much money for the United States. So riddled are the laws with loopholes, credits and opportunities for tax games that a simple territorial system would actually collect sixty billion dollars more over ten years. Another lesson of Ronald Reagan becomes apparent: simple saves money. If you get rid of shelters and complexity, you can afford lower taxes. Recently I spoke on a panel with former Democrat Senator (and New York Knicks All-Star) Bill Bradley. He lavishly praised Reagan for tax leadership and his wisdom in grasping this point. Who are the biggest losers when we move to a simple territorial system? Accountants and tax lawyers. Reagan was never cowed by Soviet Communists. He certainly didn't flinch when faced with accountants. Why are politicians today afraid of disgruntled bean counters? What are they going to do, jam up our fax machines?

The United States sits in the middle of a struggle. We are blessed with entrepreneurs, many of them young and full of swagger, who believe in carpe diem, seize the day. On the other side, we've got government agents and bureaucrats who spend their lives living the motto carpe *per* diem, roughly translated as "seize their money each day." Here is a question facing businesspeople: Why swim into turbulent waters, with the impossible obligations of Social Security and Medicare, along with a prejudicial worldwide tax system that penalizes American businesses for having the nerve to make a profit outside of the United States? They can search for calmer waters elsewhere.

Sure, some businesspeople are shortsighted and foolish. Nonetheless, the better ones consider not just the next quarterly report but their long-run prospects. These are the very corporations that our policy should be encouraging. Fly-by-night firms will flit about with the patience of a hummingbird, no matter what we do.

Sometime in the next fifteen years the United States will confront a pile of IOUs that sit on the shoulders of young people. Faced with rocketing tax rates and no faith in the fairness of the system, young workers will be sorely tempted to shrug off the unreasonable demands of baby boomers. They are not Atlas; they won't flinch before shrugging.

FIVE

Barriers to Entry

How Regulations Limit Competition and Cut Down Job Opportunities

Bruce Lee knew a lot about knuckles. He developed the amazing "one-inch punch," in which he would pose with his arm straight out, daring a man to stand next to his already extended fist. Then he would merely shrug his shoulder. Almost by electric force the shoulder shrug would launch into a brief but surging punch that would down the man.

Not only does Bruce Lee set an example of lightning-quick punches and mighty balletic kicks, but he also can teach us about an economic concept—barriers to entry. Lee, who was born in San Francisco but raised in Hong Kong, hated discrimination, whether it was whites turning him down for jobs or Chinese urging their brethren to turn down whites. It was 1964. Bruce was living in Oakland, teaching at his Jun Fan kung fu school. But he violated a key tenet of the Chinese martial arts society: do not teach our secrets to the Caucasians. The angry leaders of China-town's kung fu schools barged into Bruce's studio, brandished and unfurled an ornate scroll demanding that Bruce stop tutoring whites and blacks. The intimidating posse issued a threat: if Bruce did not cease, he must fight their kung fu master, Wong Jack

Man, who had recently arrived from China festooned with honorary belts. Bruce glanced at his wife, Linda (who was eight months pregnant with their son Brandon). He accepted the challenge, most certainly a vicious battle against a fierce and renowned champion.

The hulking Wong Jack Man began to set the rules for the fight: "No hitting in the face. No kicking in the groin."

Bruce refused: "You've made the challenge—so I'm making the rules. . . . It's no holds barred. It's all out!"

The fight began. Within seconds Bruce's rapid punches pummeled and disoriented Wong Jack Man. The master from China backpedaled. Bruce followed him with kicks, and then Wong Jack Man actually turned his back on Bruce and began to run away. Bruce dragged him into the center of the ring again. Angered and embarrassed, Wong's students entered the ring to help their beleaguered master. Bruce's friend James blocked their entrance as Bruce beat Wong to the ground.

Bruce raised his fist over Wong's face: "Is that enough?"

"That's enough!" pleaded Wong, who later claimed that Bruce tried to gouge out his eyes.[1]

That was as much as the martial arts community could stand as they retreated from Bruce Lee's studio and left him free to teach his magic to anyone he wanted.

What's the lesson for us? The martial arts teachers of Chinatown had formed a trade coalition, not much different from a medieval guild or from the California Bar Association today. The dojo gurus did not create a free trade coalition but a collusive, anti-free trade cartel. Like most guilds, one of their chief purposes was to repress and coerce competitors, for example, to prevent some newcomer off the boat from Hong Kong from shaking up their cozy traditional relationships. Economists have been harping about this since Adam Smith condemned apprenticeship rules. Smith pointed out a number of absurdities, for instance: English coach makers were prohibited from making wheels, yet wheelmakers could build coaches to place on top of the four wheels they made![2] Trade groups love peace and calm. They hate renegades. They have nightmares about new sources of competition that can destroy traditional profit margins. When the Japanese economy finally opened up to international competition in the 1990s, Japanese consumers finally got bargains and stopped paying fifteen dollars for a grapefruit. What did Japanese businessmen call this phenomenon? "Price destruction." Remember the panic at neighborhood booksellers in the United States during the early 1990s, when Borders opened up megastores, which was only exceeded by the panic at Borders when Amazon.com suddenly appeared on screens. Of course, the neighborhood stores lacked the market muscle to block out new competitors. Because bookstores, whether built of bricks or bytes, compete so aggressively we all get big discounts from official list prices. Nobody pays retail anymore (though you can make an exception in the case of this book).

Alliances or Obstacles?

The biggest problem for consumers and for the economy comes not from informal ties and alliances among businesses. You can't blame people working in a similar line of business for fraternizing and comparing notes. Throughout Las Vegas, New Orleans and Orlando, business associations are meeting in hotels to discuss legitimate strategies and the latest technologies. When I worked at the White House, the Public Liaison office asked me to give a speech to the Anti-Friction League. When I confessed that I wasn't necessarily against friction, they informed me that it was the association of ball-bearing makers. The problem arises, however, when the government intrudes and helps incumbent businesses block new competitors. Nobel Laureate George Stigler called this the capture theory of regulation, for the regulated industry ends up capturing the bureaucrats.[3] There is a big difference between merely slipping a private membership card into your wallet, saying you have paid your dues to the Association of Street Sweepers and having the government set up roadblocks to stop someone else from joining the crew.

How does this work? Consider a state's board of barbers. The board insists on certain rules and standards—for example, all barbers must sterilize their combs and reject any customers who look like cocker spaniels. These rules may slightly raise costs, but the barbers may persuade the board to adopt other rules that may benefit them grandly, especially by restricting entry. The board may hinder new barbers from moving to the state by demanding that they spend a year in Jamaica cutting Rastafarian dreadlocks or that they intern at a minimum wage for three years at an accredited dandruff clinic. These regulations, aimed at protecting barbers from competition, are offered under the guise of protecting the public against putting scissors in the hands of clumsy novices. In fact, the public gets scalped.

Here's a real-life example. Ms. Essence Farmer spent three years performing African-style hair-braiding in Maryland. Then the twenty-three-year-old came up with an idea: why not move close to her parents in Phoenix and open up her own shop? That's when she learned about Arizona's twisted hair braiding regulations. The state demanded that hairstylists take sixteen hundred hours of classroom instruction—at a cosmetology school approved by the government. The cost? Ten thousand dollars. That's not the outrageous part. Apparently, of the sixteen hundred hours, not one would be devoted to African hair braiding.[4] How many hours of training does Phoenix demand of a policeman? Six hundred hours. Evidently, it takes almost three times as much training to pick up a comb than a .357 magnum. Now that you know this, do you feel safer traveling to Phoenix? Arizona seems particularly license happy. Even rainmakers must get a license. Rainmakers in arid Arizona? Forget a license. If they could just conjure up a sweat, I'd give them a free spa visit to the Biltmore Hotel.

The Licensing Epidemic

Unfortunately, more and more American jobs have become licensed and subject to all sorts of government restrictions. Over fifty years ago Milton Friedman's dissertation warned that in "all professions . . . aristocratic, or at least restrictive movement" had taken hold. In 1900 just more than 4 percent of the labor force worked in professional occupations, but by midcentury "there were more than 1,200 state occupational licensing statutes, averaging 25 per state, for at least 75 occupations ranging from physicians to embalmers."[5] From cradle to grave an American passed through the hands of licensed professionals.

With every decade that passes, we ratchet up the number of licenses and close down opportunities for fresh and hungry young workers. Today, more than 18 percent of the workforce requires a license, covering eight hundred different jobs. That is much more than the total number of union jobs in the country. In New York one needs a license simply to fix a VCR so it stops blinking "12:00," to work as an usher on Broadway, or even to sell tickets at a wrestling match.[6] The wrestlers may be total frauds pretending to body slam their three-hundred-pound steroid-injected bodies, but you might need to pass a real test to pass out a paper ticket!

How does this overlicensing shape the outsourcing debate? By insisting on silly, expensive and arduous licenses, the government prevents Americans from entering well-paying professions and getting good jobs. Licensed jobs tend to be service jobs that require human contact. They are often difficult to outsource. Outsourcing thrives on jobs that do not require a close human connection, but can be done simply through electrons pulsing their way across cables, wires and antennae. Therefore, licensed jobs often present good job opportunities for American workers. However, the licensing requirements keep down the number of Americans who can perform those jobs. Our free trade system allows service jobs to be outsourced. That's okay. But we should have free trade in domestic service jobs, not one that is rigged to keep down the number of workers. By allowing free trade in foreign jobs but rigging trade in domestic jobs, we rob Americans of job opportunities. Workers who lose their jobs to outsourcing sometimes feel that the government is leaving them with just crumbs, or crummy jobs. The occupational licensing epidemic encourages that resentment. If we could liberate more jobs from the epidemic, we could open up more opportunities for jobs at home.

Why do we have these rules? Friedman pointed out that in the nineteenth century we acknowledged only three learned professions: medicine, law and theology. Now, somehow, everybody is a professional. I'm not sure whether it was comedians or bureaucrats who began calling garbagemen sanitation engineers, but the trend has been in place for quite a while now. It raises self-esteem, but it also can raise prices, by raising barriers to entry. In the music world, orchestra conductors have been called maestro and professor for a long time. It does take a lot of talent and training to keep the William Tell Overture from galloping away from you. I have no gripe with such honorary titles. But in North Carolina, a quick-witted, quick-thinking person cannot auction property without obtaining an official license from the Auctioneer Licensing Board. You could be auctioneering a sorry looking lot of busted bicycles and broken bed frames and still face a stiff fine if you do not post your certificate. With everyone claiming to be a professional, I'm reminded of Jackie Mason's routine about Hollywood, where everyone he meets claims to be a producer and says "Here's my card."

"What do you produce?"

"Oh, well, I'm going to," they stutter. "I almost did, I have this project that might, someday . . . well, my card says 'producer.' "

"I've figured out what they produce," Mason says. "Business cards. That's it."

We produce self-esteem by wiping out jobs.

Defending the License

The classic defense of official government licensing is simple: we are protecting the public from unqualified, unscrupulous opportunists. It is not a thoroughly stupid argument, and it seems most persuasive when talking about surgeons and other people who might touch your internal organs with sharp implements. Issuing special licenses gives providers an incentive to invest in more study and gives more confidence to insurance companies.

But more than surgical gloves separate a brain surgeon from, say, a fortune-teller—yet Arizona demands a license for both! Professor Morris M. Kleiner of the University of Minnesota has studied licensing for years and reports that in New Mexico a house painter will lose his license if he paints only one wall rather than four walls of a room—even if the customer wants him to stop at one.[7] Apparently, it is someone else's job to paint just one wall.

While the "public safety" argument makes some intuitive sense, it looks flimsy when considering two retorts: First, it should apply only to narrow, life-threatening professions and cannot explain the explosion of government licensing covering nearly one-fifth of the workforce. Second, numerous studies have shown that government licensing does little or nothing to enhance quality or safety. Meanwhile, it drives up the costs to consumers and drives down the job opportunities for those who want to enter the field. In Massachusetts three times as many jobs require licenses as in Rhode Island.[8] Should you wear a helmet and Kevlar vest when you cross the border into lenient Rhode Island?

If you eliminate licensing, does that mean consumers are on their own, at the mercy of quacks and snake oil salesmen? No. Instead of government licenses, which force the government to arrest or fine nonlicense holders, state governments could still offer examinations and issue public certificates stating the test scores or the level of skill demonstrated.[9] Then the consumer could choose whether or not to give her business to a certified practitioner. But it would not be illegal for a consumer to hire someone who did not have the certificate or who did not score well. In the real world, licensing boards tend to be stacked with practitioners who have a vested interest in preventing competition. And occupations that wield a lot of political power seem to win the toughest regulations for themselves.[10] As George Stigler warned, however, even when licensing boards add more "public citizens," they often guard the interests of the status quo practitioners anyway. Across the globe we see that those countries that put up the biggest barriers to entry tend to fuel the most corruption, the least democracy and the biggest black markets. Moreover, they destroy jobs, especially for young people.[11]

Harming the Consumer

How does the consumer get harmed in licensing? Four basic ways: first, by cutting back the supply of workers, the consumer has to pay more money for the service.

Second, as the lack of competition pushes up prices, the consumer may not be able to afford the work and may try to perform it himself. Believe it or not, some hapless individuals have actually tried to give themselves a root canal rather than visit the dentist![12] Comedian Steven Wright said he installed a skylight in his apartment. "The people who live above me are furious." With so few licensed electricians and craftsmen, it might happen.

Third, overqualified professionals refuse to make room for less qualified people who could do the job just as well. In Tempe, Arizona, a teenage entrepreneur named Christian Alf smelled a rat. In response to reports of rodents, Alf started a business installing wire mesh over vents and pipes to stop rats from moving into attics. Then the Arizona Structural Pest Control jumped into the scene, threatening the young man with a thousand-dollar fine if he did not stop stopping the rats. Happily, Alf's story made headlines in Tempe, rattling the control board, which ultimately backed down from its cease and desist order. The point here is that the simple task of nailing wire mesh was deemed too professional for an unlicensed amateur. Liberated from the silly rules, Alf has built a business and has hired friends and charges thirty dollars per house for his service. The *Arizona Republic* quotes Alf: "Most of the people I get are elderly single people. But I am now starting to get quite a few people who just don't have time." He reports that he's learned a great deal from his "entrepreneurial venture, including the basics of scheduling appointments, managing employees that are older than he is and stocking supplies."[13] In sum, more jobs at less cost. And fewer rats.

Fourth, as repressed competition lifts prices, it discourages people from visiting as often, leaving them more vulnerable to damage. If only a high-cost licensed inspector can snoop around your house looking for termites, you might neglect to hire an inspector on a regular basis.

Of course, it is not just the consumer who loses. The job seeker loses the chance to work and earn an honest living. Licensing costs consumers and workers in another way, too. By keeping out entrants, it limits people from moving from county to county or from state to state. A smooth-functioning economy should make it easier to look for work and easier for resources to move to where they are most needed. If workers were not forced to get a new license every time they tried to move to another state, it would boost mobility by 60 percent, concluded Kleiner.[14] Now, this can easily turn into a federalism debate, wherein each state argues that its laws should prevail. I have a great respect for federalism and for Justice Louis Brandeis's famous dissent in *New State Ice Co.* v. *Liebmann,* in which he lauds states as the "laboratories" of democracy, each able to conduct its own policy tests. Nonetheless, states should recognize that when they insist on erecting barriers to entry, they are mostly hurting their own citizens. The Supreme Court will soon decide whether states can block wine from crossing state lines. The case pits the Constitution's commerce clause against the Twenty-first Amendment, which ended Prohibition and gave power to the states. Scholars may disagree on the legal points, but economists know that a more fluid wine market would lower prices for wine drinkers and create jobs for those who like to stomp on grapes, or at least, transport the tasty fruit juice.

Over the past twenty years European economies have generally lagged the U.S. economy because their restrictions have reenforced encrusted provincial jobs and prevented young people from relocating. Slowly Europe and Japan have begun to recognize the illogic of excessive regulation, especially as the European Union has tried to reconcile the combined millions of national rules covering all trades and practices. A recent study of French retailers offers an interesting lesson. Starting in 1974 France began protecting small retail stores from the "unruly" growth of big stores. So regional zoning boards began turning down applications for large new shops. The crackdown did not apply to hotels and restaurants. What happened? Retail job creation skidded to a smoky halt. Meanwhile, hotel and restaurant jobs grew steadily. By protecting incumbent store owners, the government actually took away job opportunities from workers, especially younger ones.[15]

Jobs, Jobs, Jobs

Let's now look at some of the other occupations where we erect barriers to entry and drive up prices. We'll examine the impact of the barriers and the issues of quality, safety and cost. Though I have shared with you some some bizarre examples, from the fortune-teller to the rainmaker, occupational licensing is a serious problem that prevents millions of American people from getting the job they want. Let's start with the people who take care of our teeth.

Dentists

Do you need a dentist to watch over the shoulder of a dental hygienist who cleans your teeth? Why can't a dental hygienist open up an office, offering cleaning services? The hygienist could encourage you to see a dentist on a regular basis for more thorough exams. But in the meantime, your teeth may sparkle just as brightly at a lower cost. A study in the *Journal of Law and Economics* compared dental costs in states with restrictive licensing with those with a more lenient approach. Of twelve common dental procedures, eleven cost more in states with restrictive licensing. That shows up in dentists' incomes, of course, as they earn about 12 percent more in highly regulated states, costing consumers several billion dollars. Compared with workers with similar educations but without the benefit of restrictive licensing, dentists earn about 30 percent more. We know that this extra money buys dentists BMWs and time shares in Florida, but does the extra money buy anything for the patient? Apparently not. Several careful studies have demonstrated that quality does not suffer when dental licensing rules are relaxed. The same results apparently hold in Canada, where the province of Saskatchewan concluded that modern dentistry can rely much more on hygienists and paraprofessionals, which could push down costs by 30 percent to 40 percent. One study made an even stronger, more worrisome argument: by cutting off the supply of dentists and making appointments more expensive, tough licensing leads many people to neglect their teeth, for example, older people with ill-fitting dentures.[16]

Medical Doctors

The AMA used to be more blunt about its motives. At its first convention in 1847 it declared: "The very large number of physicians in the United States . . . has frequently been the subject of remark. To relieve the diseases of something more than twenty millions of people, we have an army of doctors amounting by a recent computation to forty thousand, which allows one to about every five hundred inhabitants. And if we add to the 40,000 the long list of irregular practitioners who swarm like locusts in every part of the country, the proportion of patients will be still further reduced. No wonder, then, that the profession of medicine has measurably ceased to occupy the elevated position which once it did; no wonder that the merest pittance in the way of remuneration is scantily doled out even to the most industrious in our ranks. . . ."

So the enemy was more doctors and the symptom was less income. In 1888, the *Journal of the American Medical Association* declared that "wholesome competition is the life of trade; unrestricted competition may be the death of it." In 1898, New York's medical society tried to stop free vaccination and free diphtheria antitoxin claiming that it was *"inimic to the best welfare of young medical men* [italics added]."[17] In colonial times clergymen like Cotton Mather fought for smallpox inoculations, mostly debating doctors.

Now that we know what kept doctors up at night, we can also understand why they tried to stamp out competition from any unlicensed person and revised the definition of medicine to bar nontraditional types like osteopaths, chiropractors and even Christian Scientists. The courts enforced the barriers and it did not matter whether the patients got better from chiropractors or died at the hands of official, traditional MDs. This at a time when AMA-approved surgeons roamed the country, slicing open patients without even bothering to wash their hands! (Joseph Lister and Louis Pasteur had not yet taught them how.)

In the early twentieth century the AMA took control of medical schools, leading to a rapid drop in the number of institutions and the ratio of doctors to population from 1900 to about 1940. Schools that accepted women were shuttered, along with most that trained African Americans.

In recent years, doctors have had a tougher time controlling alternative medicine. King Lear said a thankless child is "sharper than a serpent's tooth." Doctors feel the same way about an acupuncturist's needle or a Chinese herbalist's ginseng root. Physicians who live in states that do not severely limit alternative medicines earn significantly lower incomes than those in more restrictive licensing regimes.[18]

Even sticking with traditional medicines, most honest family doctors will tell you that much of their day is "cookbook" medicine. A kid comes in with a sore throat. Take a strep culture and give him a pain reliever. A man has a headache. Give him aspirin and ask him to come back for more serious tests if the symptoms linger. Chest pains? Check his vital signs and history and then send him to a cardiologist. Perhaps 80 percent of pediatrics can be competently performed by highly qualified nurses, at far less cost, suggests one judicious report.[19] Many rural areas and inner cities cannot afford to wait for high-priced, gold-plated specialists.

Sometimes medical professionals get into a slugfest among themselves. The State of California has obstructed oral surgeons from performing cosmetic surgery on the face. Plastic surgeons are furious that the restriction may be lifted, allowing mere dental professionals to pick up a scalpel. It is indeed a rare occurrence when restrictions get erased. (Another example came in Minnesota, which lifted licensing for watchmakers when the number of watchmakers dropped to under one hundred.)

"The whole thing is so audacious that I have trouble controlling myself . . . this is just, just, just, I mean, it's offensive, incredible," said Dr. Harvey A. Zarem, a leading plastic surgeon and occasional guest on ABC-TV's inoffensive and tasteful *Extreme Makeover* show.

Oral surgeons disagree, of course. "Let's say you are in a horrible accident and half your face is torn off," one explained. "I can reattach it and then do all the followup surgeries to make sure it looks perfect. . . . I can go in and reattach someone's nose in the middle of the night." But if the nose grew up to be crooked or you were born with a lopsided grin, he cannot help.[20]

This is a battle royal over the vanity of California baby boomers. It pits the rich versus the affluent. But why shouldn't a consumer have the choice to consult with and pick one kind of surgeon rather than another? The argument for choice has become even stronger in recent years because the Internet places in our hands more information than anyone has ever had. Doctor friends tell me that patients are reading everything from the Men's Health Web site to professional medical journals before they walk into their clinic or slip into a drafty hospital gown.

Now, of course, there is misinformation on the net, too, but consumers are certainly better suited to make judgments than ever in human history.

Eye Care

Do you want to pay more for your eyes? Simple: go to a state that piles on tough license restrictions and prevents you from buying contact lenses unless you recently renewed your prescription. Hefty licensing requirements drive up eye exams and eyeglass prescription costs by one-third.[21] California won't let you buy contact lenses from an 800 contact lens company unless you have a prescription less than one year old. The contact lens company is forced to snoop around, calling your optometrist to verify that you are telling the truth. Eye care professionals hate advertising. No surprise, because advertising has cut the cost of high margin eyeglasses.[22] Looser licensing would give consumers an even better deal while providing more job opportunities.

Beauty Culture

Earlier I described the case of Essence Farmer, who wanted to hair braid in Arizona without paying a ten-thousand-dollar tuition bill and spending sixteen hundred hours receiving instruction. Compared with Oregon, sixteen hundred hours may be a bargain for that state recently boosted its requirement from fifteen hundred hours to twenty-five hundred hours. The official state auditor of Hawaii has studied whether any of this made sense, especially in a state with a small population. Hawaii has been regulating barbering since 1947 and beauty culture since 1929. The auditor has issued five reports since 1980, all of them denouncing the regulations: "The practices of barbering and beauty culture pose a minimal risk to the public's health . . . there is little evidence of abuses by barbers and beauty culturists . . . regulation of barbering and beauty culture reduces the number of individuals able to provide services and thereby limits consumer choice. Relatively high failure rates for . . . examinations indicate that these examinations are barriers to entry . . ." A slam dunk case for repeal, right? Who would stand in the way? The auditor tells us: "the Board of Barbering and Cosmetology noted strong disagreement" and feels that repeal would "open the door to fraud, incompetence, and public distrust."[23]

Florists

If you thought beauty culture was difficult, you should try the florist business in Louisiana. Over half the people who try to become florists fail the two-part exam, which includes a written test and a hands-on design test. In the design phase, licensed professionals pick apart the arrangements that are created under tight time constraints. Do the petunias have the right focal point? Are the daisies spaced effectively? How ironic: In New Orleans, you can stumble down Bourbon Street amid lewd signs for nude dancing and the most vulgar T-shirts, but put down those tulips unless you've got a license to beautify! There is an exception, of course. Under Louisiana law you can escape the exam if you agree to sell cut flowers without arranging them in a fancy way and if you use only one kind of flower. Lonely arrangements require no license.

While we're discussing flowers, you might note that eleven states overregulate the sales of caskets, demanding that only licensed funeral directors with hundreds of hours of training sell the wooden coffins. State funeral boards are generally controlled by funeral directors, who earn a huge proportion of their profits on sales of pricey caskets. It's a somber subject, but purchasing caskets is an extremely expensive, if not bankrupting, experience for many families.

Other Trades

Researchers Sidney Carroll and Robert Gaston performed a sweeping study and concluded that licensing impedes not just quantity but quality as well. Some examples follow:[24]

Plumbers and Electricians: barriers to entry persuade more people to do it themselves. While this sounds like noble, Emersonian self-reliance, fewer available tradesmen leads to more people's electrocuting themselves and blowing up their toilets.

Real Estate Brokers: barriers reduced the quality of service and left more homes sitting longer on the market unsold. Around the country today, real estate licensing boards are trying to shut down Internet-based realty firms, which offer lower commission rates, often half as much as conventional brokerage arrangements.[25] The Internet has empowered home buyers so that they have more precise and timely information about mortgage rates, recent home price sales, as well as local ordinances. With a click of a mouse or tap of a touch pad, a prospective buyer can comparison shop for mortgage rates and financing terms.[26] Unfortunately, our licensing rules can discourage this efficient behavior as they try to protect the sixty-billion-dollar pot of commissions.

Veterinarians: barriers reduce the number of vets, driving up their incomes but leaving more animals suffering from rabies.

Mr. Trump: "You're Fired"

Donald Trump and NBC have earned stellar ratings for *The Apprentice* and for Mr. Trump's melodramatic declaration "You're fired." In truth, these days almost no one gets fired in such direct terms. To borrow Thomas Hobbes's phrase, Mr. Trump's dismissal is too nasty, too brutish and too short. Besides, it could lead to a harassment suit. In addition to ladling license regulations on our job market, courts and governments have also added "wrongful termination" rules intended to protect a worker from being fired without good reason. Here again we often see lawyers disagreeing with economists. Numerous economic studies have shown that such termination protections actually hurt job seekers by forcing employers to throw away more money on screening potential employees and paying off disgruntled workers and their lawyers. The word "severance," once reserved for the elites, has entered common parlance. A corporate counsel will urge the boss to pay severance as long as he can get the terminated person to sign a release and agree not to drag the firm into court. Firms increasingly deal with expensive wrongful termination rules in a more sly way, too: they hire temporary workers, 14 percent to 22 percent more than they otherwise would, according to one report. About five hundred thousand temps might be denied full-time jobs because their employers want to preserve some flexibility in the face of rigid termination rules.[27] Most interesting, the federal government, which insulates itself from many of these rules, slashed its temp force from about 40 percent in 1982 to almost zero in 1997.[28] A study by the nonpartisan Rand Institute calculated that wrongful termination rules sliced payrolls by 2 percent to 5 percent.[29]

Would more protection be even better? No one gets more protection than a French or German worker who can get paid for hardly working. In one recent scandal, a German man was collecting unemployment compensation even while retired in a Miami condominium. European entrepreneurs complain that hiring someone is like adopting a son. Just as you cannot send the kid back to the orphanage, you cannot get rid of a bad worker. So you think twice, or thrice or forever before extending a job offer. That's why the European jobless rate struggled to get below 10 percent during the booming 1990s, even as the U.S. rate fell to under 4 percent. A similar picture shows up in India, where a study showed that pro-worker legal acts actually incited lower investment, fewer jobs and less manufacturing output.[30] The problem with socialism is that it gives everyone a bed but no reason to get out of it. Unfortunately, the same can be said of irrational labor laws even if they are promulgated under democratic capitalism.

License to Kill

By pretending that 18 percent of the U.S. job market needs government approval, we are blocking the on-ramp for people to enter the workforce or change to better jobs. We are taking away opportunities for people who have lost jobs to outsourcing. In short, we have given government—in cahoots with incumbent professionals—a "license to kill" jobs. Considering the voluminous empirical studies, I would calculate that this ever-expanding trend costs our economy about five million to ten million job

slots. If we add in the damage from courts' inventing and enforc-
ing wrongly termination terms, that number moves higher by
several million. Most galling, of course, is that America would
not become less safe, just less expensive and more inviting to
people who have been struggling to find good jobs.

Remember the old song, "Mamas, Don't Let Your Babies
Grow Up to Be Cowboys"? To update that song, you would have
to unfurl a whole scroll of warnings, including everything from
plumbers to television repairmen to florists. At the rate we're going, being a cowboy may be the only place left for a guy who
doesn't want to stand in line waiting for a ticket at the government's licensing counter.

SIX

Jobs v. Lawyers

How Litigation Kills Jobs

If Philadelphia was known for lawyers in 1776, it would have sued the makers of the Liberty Bell, melted it down and then filed a claim in Concord to repossess Paul Revere's horse. Today's litigation stories are, paradoxically, more trivial and yet more dangerous. Hot coffee from McDonald's yields a $2.7 million verdict. The courts oversee a $3.75 million settlement paid by Hooters restaurant to a few men who applied for work and could not fill out the Hooters' costume. Meanwhile, the Supreme Court embarrasses itself by opining on whether a male football coach may pat a player on the rump without raising fears of sexual harassment. A blind woman threatens to sue the National Symphony Orchestra because she wants her Seeing Eye dog to enter their fund-raiser, a decorator show house. What decorating tips, may I ask, would the blind woman or her dog see in the house?

It would be easier, of course, if we did not have civil disputes. But ever since Noah guided some pairs of animals and not others aboard his boat, we've had civil disagreements and disturbances. So what's new? Two things: First, the sheer magnitude of precious resources—brainpower, time and money—we waste on litigation. In the United States we spend more than two hundred billion dollars each year fighting and defending against one another in courtrooms. That's half the size of the Pentagon's annual budget for defending us against terrorism, missiles and foreign armies. A study of international manufacturers concluded that excessive litigation grants foreign firms a 3.2 percent cost advantage over U.S.-based firms.[1] Second, the tactics have changed. Lawyers can enrich themselves so lavishly that they have enormous incentives to undermine firms, shareholders and employees. These two factors kill productive jobs and persuade firms to move jobs away from the fifty states and to friendlier climes.

I also worry about the unmeasurable social costs and the decay of common decency and honesty. In 1993, the State of New Jersey conducted an experiment, staging a bogus bus accident. Normally, a vehicle accident incites passengers to hurry off the vehicle, fleeing for safety. In this case, however, hidden cameras captured on video seventeen people scrambling to board the bus before the police arrived. When the police arrived, many wailed and all of them claimed to be injured. Two other people later filed suit—and they had never gotten near the bus! They had not even bothered or been able to scramble aboard. Nice work if you can get it, I suppose. But the brand of work shows how pernicious the litigation craze has grown.

In this chapter we will uncover the seamy side of litigation and assess the damage done to job prospects in America. Then we can suggest some reforms, all the while being careful not to offend anyone, lest I be named in a libel suit.

Luck Be a Lady Tonight

Imagine you could cut out all the risk in life. Wouldn't that be nice! No need to buy that health insurance policy because you know you're going to live to one hundred. And even better, your favorite baseball team will win the World Series ten times in a row. (It must have been great to be a Yankee fan in the 1920s.) Don't bother getting to the airport early, because there won't be any traffic and your plane will be taking off right on time! Oh, and that promotion you were hoping for, which would catapult you to the corner office? Yep, you got it.

Okay, how did you like heaven on earth? What a bore. It's not living; it's just playing the role of a Barbie or Ken doll, smiling like a boob. It also reminds me of the Bill Murray movie *Groundhog Day,* where the weatherman finds himself repeating the exact day, again and again and again. No risk of rain because it didn't rain yesterday and the weatherman is always right.

Yet our legal culture tries to exalt this as a goal: to eliminate all risk and to achieve certainty. If you fail to achieve that promised result, you should sue for a fortune. We were a lot better off when people blamed God, the devil, Lady Luck or Richard Nixon for all their problems. You can't bring those defendants into a courtroom and gum up the economy.

If tort lawyers had been waiting for the Pilgrims on Plymouth Rock, the Mayflower Compact would have been two hundred pages long and filled with disclaimers and escape clauses. Heck, the Pilgrims never would have left Europe, and Columbus's crew would have sued him for promising a cruise to India and instead delivering the Bahamas.

Today most people have no understanding of the concept of risk and an infantile understanding of what kind of behavior is most risky. I have several friends who are frightened of flying, but spend most of their days carpooling their kids on the roads and freeways. And when they plan a vacation? A driving trip to a historical place like Williamsburg, surrounded by outlet shopping malls! Another friend, thanks to the Atkins diet, looks at a bread roll like Dracula looks at a crucifix, but thinks nothing of hopping in a taxi driven by some guy who just got off the boat from a country that hasn't yet invented the traffic light.

ABC's John Stossel performed a Geraldo-like dialogue with his audience, asking them to pretend they were government regulators. Would they approve certain products? Suppose he presented a "new" toy, a recreational device . . .

"but it [would] kill[s] six hundred Americans a year and leave one thousand others with brain damage. Anyone know what this is?"

A PARTICIPANT: A plastic bag?

STOSSEL: Plastic bags. No, they kill a couple of dozen a year.

A PARTICIPANT: Lead poisoning.

STOSSEL: Lead poisoning. No.

A PARTICIPANT: Bicycling.

STOSSEL: Bicycles. No. Swimming pools . . . would swimming pools be approved today? Would cars be approved today? I want to invent a new device that will . . . weigh a ton, and we're going to drive them inches from pedestrians. It would never be approved. And we're going to let sixteen-year-olds drive them.

Stossel also challenged the audience with statistics on natural gas. Would the EPA, FDA and other regulators approve a super-flammable explosive to be pumped into people's homes, knowing it would kill four hundred people each year from explosions and carbon monoxide poisoning?[2]

We cannot erase all risks. Every time we build a bridge or tunnel, someone dies building it, whether from an accident or a heart attack. Should we never stray from home? Without the Golden Gate Bridge, San Franciscans might still get to Marin County, but on ferries. Can you make failproof ferries? Only if God makes failproof weather, and so far He shows no signs of bestowing it on San Francisco. Mark Twain knew that when he stated that the coldest winter he ever spent was summer in that beautiful, foggy city.

You Can't Hide from the Class Action Crisis

Even if you promise never to sue, never to go to a courtroom and never even to watch *The Practice* on television, you cannot avoid the liability crisis. This is especially true when you consider the position of shareholders and employees. Let's face it, it is not easy to be an investor in America today, though most families do own shares in the equity market. How do you sort out the daily barrage of financial reports and the endless babble of market "experts"? An investor can try to studiously follow a firm as it confronts a turbulent business climate: Is the firm meeting its sales goals? Is it preparing to float another stock offering or taking on more debt? Is the new advertising campaign working or backfiring? These are challenging hurdles for the most battle-tested professional money managers. Even if the investor clears these high hurdles, there are more hurdles ahead. For example, how's the economy doing? Is the Federal Reserve Board clamping down on growth or juicing it up? Does it matter if the value of the U.S. dollar slides? Or if the price of oil jumps up? Do you have to watch CNBC twenty-four hours a day or else feel guilty for neglecting your nest egg?

Considering all the risks—all the financial asteroids streaming past their portfolios—we should applaud the majority of American families who are willing to take up the challenge and brave the equity markets.

Entrepreneurs, too, are eager to confront these questions and to jump over the expected hurdles. If they succeed, they and their investors will be enriched. At the same time, investors recognize that by buying shares in companies, they take a risk that the entrepreneurs and corporate managers may fail to meet these challenges. For the millions of American families who invest in stocks and bonds, it seems like a fair deal that has built up the American economy, indeed the American dream.

But in recent years a new and troubling stumbling block has emerged to stand in the way of business success and investor gains. The usual suspects did not build this new stumbling block. It did not arise from wily competitors, volatile stock markets, the fickleness of consumer tastes or even the caprice of government regulators. Instead, this latest and dangerous foe shows up at a company's doorstep in the form of a filing for a class action lawsuit, a lawyer's document alleging an infinite variety of corporate misjudgments and missteps. Like the catalyst embedded in a nuclear explosive, the arrival of this document can ignite a chain of events that damages the financial standing of the corporation and the well-being of its shareholders. Bond ratings may sink, borrowing costs may rise, goodwill and reputation may suffer and share prices may sink. In a single day in September 1999, shareholders in HMOs watched twelve billion dollars of their assets wiped out after plaintiffs' lawyers breathlessly described their plan of attack to Wall Street analysts.

Sometimes there are legitimate victims of corporate negligence and malfeasance. And, of course, they should be fairly compensated for their losses. I don't dispute the principle that victims should have the power to sue businesses. Instead, I argue that: the legal system unduly encourages unwarranted class action lawsuits, which are seldom decided in a courtroom on their merits; shareholders, taxpayers, consumers and workers and job seekers all suffer from this lawsuit abuse; and tort lawyers have tremendous incentives to exacerbate the damage to shareholders in order to squeeze firms for the largest possible settlements. I will also point out how tort lawyers disproportionately benefit compared with their class action clients. By the end of this chapter, you may wonder, "Why would anyone hire Americans when less litigious people are eager to work elsewhere?"

Myth: Investors Can Hide from Unwarranted Litigation

American businesses are virtually stalked by class action tort lawyers. They advertise on television, in the newspapers and in the subway cars of our cities. "Have you bought a car made by . . . ?" "Have you ever used . . . medication?" "Click here if you or someone you know has a loan with . . ." Suing corporations has turned into a lucrative and brutal contact sport, not just a spectator sport, as tort lawyers try to gather as big a plaintiff's class as possible. The U.S. civil liability system already costs

more than 2 percent of our gross domestic product and drives
down wages by 3 percent to 5 percent.[3] Class action lawsuits in-
tensify and spread the pain of such litigation.

Investors cannot hide from the onslaught. Consider the following statements:

- *"I don't invest directly. I buy only index funds or own stocks
  through my pension plan."*

Over the past twenty years, millions of families have embraced index funds in order to own a diversified set of equities
while holding down administrative costs. An index fund might
simply track the performance of the S&P 500 by buying shares
in proportion to the index. In my 1995 book *From Here to Economy: A Shortcut to Economic Literacy,* I advocated these vehi-
cles. But buying index funds does not insulate the investor from
the costs of a class action lawsuit. The popular Vanguard S&P
500 index fund controls over $97.4 billion in assets. Its top five
holdings (as of 2004 are General Electric Co., Microsoft Corp.,
ExxonMobil Corp., Pfizer Inc. and Wal-Mart Stores, Inc.)—all
defendants in class action lawsuits. Just because someone is a
passive investor does not mean that they should passively watch
their portfolio picked apart by avaricious lawyers. Moreover,
these leading firms tend to pay higher dividends than smaller
firms and therefore frequently find themselves in the portfolios
of retirees and widows and orphans, who require regular income.

- *"I don't invest in polluters or cigarette makers."*

Some shareholders and consumers engage in "social" investing and "social shopping," deliberately avoiding firms they believe sell products that harm people, animals, the environment,
and so on. Investors have placed more than two hundred billion

dollars in mutual funds that attempted to screen out sinful firms and instead allocated money to more virtuous companies that promote an animal rights or human rights agenda. In a style labeled "rain forest chic" firms such as Ben & Jerry's, The Body Shop, Starbucks Coffee and Tom's of Maine advertise their commitment to progressive causes. In the canned food aisle of our grocery stores, StarKist advertises "dolphin-free tuna." While it is true that dolphins can escape the cans, no investor can escape the threat of unfounded lawsuits. They are filed not just against the controversial firms that arouse public protests or congressional scrutiny. Even firms admired for their environmental records can find themselves in the crosshairs of a battalion of tort lawyers. Starbucks, for example, often wins applause for providing health benefits to employees and giving customers a recycling discount for using a reusable cup. Furthermore, the company buys "fair trade" coffee beans from organic growers living near the rain forests in South America. Despite the chic pedigree, Starbucks could not fend off an expensive class action lawsuit for sex, age and disability discrimination.

- *"I don't invest in stocks."*

Surely an individual who avoids the stock market can avoid class action lawsuits, right? Wrong. When class action lawyers attack a firm for an allegedly faulty product or service, bond prices generally fall along with stock prices. The risk of a huge jury award or settlement can push a firm to the brink of bankruptcy— or beyond. Companies like Moody's and Standard & Poor's rate companies that issue bonds based on their ability to pay back the principal and interest. When the risk of a big payout to plaintiffs goes up, the risk of a default to bondholders jumps up, too. Therefore, even investors who see themselves as passive and have deliberately ignored the volatile equity market can suddenly find red ink staining their retirement savings accounts.

- *"I don't invest at all. I must spend all of my income."*

As I will discuss later, consumers also feel the pain of unwarranted class action litigation. A firm that is shoved into bankruptcy court may no longer be able to compete for a consumer's business. Faced with less competition, the surviving sellers may be able to raise the price they charge consumers for a product or service. Moreover, class action lawsuits can intimidate firms into withdrawing or delaying innovative products, cutting down the consumer's choice of goods and services.

In sum, the class action lawsuit "business" is like a tank turret that can turn 360 degrees and is able to aim at any kind of company and damage nearly any kind of investor or consumer.

The Tidal Wave of Class Action Litigation

As we are driving down the street or just sitting in our homes, we see the defendants in a class action lawsuit: Burger King (for giving away Pokémon toys), the Ralph Lauren Outlet Stores (for allegedly marking up the retail price label), Wal-Mart (for alleged labor violations in developing countries). Even Fruit of the Loom underwear has been dragged into federal court for alleged SEC violations against shareholders. Over the past ten years lawsuits have become more numerous and more lucrative for plaintiffs' lawyers. Tort costs have climbed from 1.03 percent of GDP in 1960 to 1.53 percent in 1980 to 2.23 percent in 2002.[4] Insurance premiums that protect managers from shareholder suits have raced ahead at an even faster pace. All this might seem like great news for insurance companies except that they themselves are so frequently targeted for legal attack.

Why has suing corporations grown into a kind of national sport? In short, lawyers have tremendous incentives to file lawsuits. At the same time, corporations have tremendous incentives to settle those suits, rather than plod through lengthy, expensive and risky trials. The incentives for trial lawyers are obvious in a class action lawsuit. By corralling as large a class as possible, the lawyers can allege damages that can add up to a multimillion- or even multibillion-dollar figure. By signing up as many plaintiffs as possible in a class action, tort lawyers can more easily intimidate a corporation into settling before trial. It may be easier to draw a corporation to the bargaining table for a one-billion-dollar case than a one-hundred-thousand-dollar case. A settlement or favorable verdict can make a team of attorneys very wealthy indeed. Winning lawyers can quickly jump to the first-class cabins of society or even buy their own private jets. *BusinessWeek* magazine has called $25 billion a "conservative" estimate of plaintiff-lawyer annual income, based on data from the Internal Revenue Service and the Association of Trial Lawyers of America (ATLA). Outside of winning a state lottery, winning a class action lawsuit is one of the few tickets to superrich living. It is like winning *Who Wants to Be a Millionaire* without facing off against Regis Philbin.

Toshiba settled a lawsuit for between $1 billion and $2 billion. What was the claim? That under some unusual circumstances its laptops could possibly corrupt data. How many customers actually complained about this defect? None. Certainly the plaintiffs' lawyers did not complain after grabbing their $147.5 million share of the prize. Justice Sandra Day O'Connor lamented that the system has "made more overnight millionaires than almost any other business."

The mantra of the class action plaintiff's lawyer is "Escalate! Escalate!" That is, boost the size of class, the size of damages and the threat to the corporation's reputation. The bigger the case, the bigger the payout, and the bigger the intimidation. Tort lawyers have a strong incentive to threaten the standing of a firm among Wall Street analysts. If they can trigger a flurry of stock selling, they can trigger a serious settlement discussion.

Technology has made it easier for lawyers to organize classes and to share information and strategies. Lawyers have effectively deployed Internet tools to launch multistate attacks on firms. No longer do tort lawyers slave away in lonely, dim-lit libraries at midnight to uncover old depositions and to discover expert witnesses. Instead they may log on to Web sites set up by ATLA and the Attorney Information Exchange Group (aieg.com) to share valuable litigation materials and tactics. Copycat lawsuits can be filed by purchasing prepackaged litigation kits, which guide enterprising lawyers through the complaint and discovery process, including a list of suggested documents to request from the corporate defendant. The ATLA exchange advertises:

> services critical to trial practice, including: Access to other members' successful complaints, memos, briefs, depositions, and other documents (many of which are often unpublished and unavailable from any other source), giving members a starting point for case acceptance and/or trial preparation.

A few years ago the Firestone Tire Tread Separation kit could be purchased for under two hundred dollars, in CD or paper for-mat. That two-hundred-dollar investment might have yielded very high returns for the lawyer who no longer has to start from ground zero. Just as laypeople have snatched up the branded *Dummies* books (e.g., *Investing for Dummies*) in the self-help section of their neighborhood bookstores, lawyers have picked up their own simple-to-understand and immensely valuable Firestone books. They buy the *Dummies* books, and we wear the fools' caps.

Sharing ideas, strategies and notes is generally not illegal or unethical. The point is that by developing handy, convenient, "paint by number" litigation kits, the plaintiff's bar drives down the cost of launching a big class action suit. By cutting the costs and boosting the potential returns, the legal system invites more litigation.

Because the cost/benefit calculus tilts in favor of plaintiffs' lawyers, a whole new financial industry has sprung up to "invest" in lawsuits. Firms such as American Asset Finance and ExpertFunding.com will provide funds to plaintiffs during litigation in exchange for owning a stake in the outcome. Like venture capitalists vetting business plans, such companies will place their money on those suits that look most promising. As in the venture capital business, one blockbuster hit will offset several smaller, losing cases. It is a sad commentary on American business life when the best investments are those that seek to destroy American businesses.

Do Plaintiffs Win?

And the plaintiffs themselves? Where do they fit in? Since the plaintiffs' lawyers often accept these class action cases on a contingency fee basis, the plaintiffs feel like free riders, believing they have nothing to lose by joining the class. As the Toshiba case showed, many of them do not even think they have suffered an injury. But when the class action notice arrives in the mail, the notice looks almost like a sweepstakes entry form. Ironically, in 1999 American Family Publishers Sweepstakes (AFP) settled a class action lawsuit alleging that it and spokesmen Dick Clark and Ed McMahon wrongly induced people to buy magazines, misleading them into thinking it would enhance their chances of winning AFP's multimillion-dollar sweepstakes. People who decided to join the class action actually got to enter two kinds of sweepstakes: First, the official ten-million-dollar lottery conducted by AFP, followed by the sweepstakes inherent in a class action lawsuit against AFP. In the end, the settling class actually got a third sweepstakes chance, because the settlement set up a special hundred-thousand-dollar prize that would be randomly awarded to ten members of the class (totaling one million dollars). The attorney general of Tennessee bragged about his role in the settlement. His office sent out letters to Tennessee families announcing:

> Congratulations! You are the winner, as a Tennessee consumer, in a settlement with American Family Publishers (AFP). . . . AFP, known for its catchy contest ads featuring celebrities Dick Clark and Ed McMahon, has agreed to pay some of the 33 states involved $1,250,000. Tennessee's share, totaling $50,000, will be used for consumer protection purposes.

Great! Now tell us how much time and money Tennessee's officials wasted in order to nab fifty thousand dollars and mail letters to its taxpayers!

Like a national sweepstakes, the odds of a class action plaintiff's actually collecting a large prize are small, especially since the legal fees and administrative costs gobble up such a large proportion of the settlements. A study of the Florida nursing home industry concluded that almost half of the claim costs paid under general and professional liability policies went directly to lawyers, leaving little for the actual class of plaintiffs.

After studying class action settlements, I'm convinced that plaintiffs should first receive a desk. Why? Because so often while the plaintiffs' lawyers receive cash, the injured and aggrieved people who hire them receive only coupons. At least a desk would allow them to keep the coupons somewhere. My desk is already too crowded, so I have random stacks of coupons spread throughout the house. My kids use them for tic-tac-toe. In a famous 1993 settlement, airlines accused of price-fixing paid $16 million in fees to plaintiffs' lawyers. What did plaintiffs typically get? Coupons for a $25 discount off a $250 flight. In this common kind of arrangement, the only way for a plaintiff to receive compensation is to do business once again with a vendor that allegedly engages in unfair business practices.

Have you ever paid a late fee to Blockbuster for a tape or DVD? In 2001, the video rental chain settled for $460 million. Plaintiffs could get up to $20 in rental coupons and $1 coupons for nonfood items. Lawyers got $9.25 million. Have you ever gotten bored reading a box of Cheerios? Keep reading next time. General Mills settled a suit over a food additive, though there was no evidence of injury. Lawyers got nearly $2 million in fees, about $2,000 per hour. Cheerios buyers got, of course, a coupon for a box of Cheerios.

Did you buy any lipstick, cologne or eye liner between 1994 and 2003? Lipstick moguls are currently battling over a settlement concerning charges that they limited discounting. A $175 million settlement would result in cosmetics makers giving away items worth $18 and $25. The lawyers would get up to $24 million. Now critics are petitioning a federal judge to stop the settlement, worried that the consumers would get stuck with "unpopular items, such as purple lipstick."[5]

With the potential fees often looking about the same size as a college endowment, plaintiffs' lawyers try not to let the findings of government regulators get in their way. In many cases, state and federal boards might have already ruled that the defendant corporation did no harm or violated no law. Nonetheless, the lawyers have tremendous incentives to "shop the case" until they can persuade a judge to hear it. For example, even though the Texas Insurance Department approved the practice of insurance companies' rounding up fees to the nearest dollar, plaintiffs' lawyers alleged that consumers were swindled and found a friendly court. I will address this problem later under the heading "State v. State."

Hush, Hush Goes the Corporation

The corporate calculus tilts in a very different direction. If the plaintiffs' mantra is "Escalate! Escalate!," the corporation's mantra is "Resolve, resolve, please, resolve." Unlike the tort bar, the corporation is not established as a legal fighting machine, finely tuned for hand-to-hand courtroom combat. The corporation is established to serve its shareholders and to generate the highest possible return on investment. The corporation generates that return in the market for goods and services, not in the courtroom. The top officers of a corporation seldom come from the ranks of tort lawyers. Some may have law degrees, but they are undoubtedly more skilled in the areas of mergers, acquisitions, finance and intellectual property than the art of the lawsuit. Second, the corporation has a keen stake in building up and protecting its reputation and goodwill. It needs to be trusted by consumers, by vendors, by financiers and by shareholders as an entity that conducts business fairly.[6] Trust creates brand loyalty among consumers and lowers financing costs for the firm. That is why firms spend so many millions of dollars on advertising. Consider some of the more famous advertising campaigns of the past fifty years: Texaco's "You can trust your car to the man who wears the star"; Prudential's "Own a piece of the rock." Banks have traditionally housed themselves in classic buildings with Greek columns because such sturdy architecture signals stability and trust. However, as soon as a class action lawsuit is filed and publicized, those columns and that reputation begin cracking as a result of allegations, accusations and the negative publicity they arouse. A single lawsuit without real merit can undermine a decade of sincere contributions to local and national charities.

On top of these risks to reputation, corporate counsel know the enormous cost of defending a case, including discovery, experts' fees and outside counsel. A savvy tort lawyer might also succeed in catching the eye of an enterprising politician, who can launch hearings in Congress or a state legislature, further straining the corporation. Even better if C-Span turns its cameras on the crusading business-busting politician. State attorneys general may also join in the fray, as we saw with the Dick Clark/Ed McMahon follies. The discovery process might dig up old memoranda buried in files that could embarrass the current managers and owners of a firm. These memoranda can quickly spread to lawyers throughout the country using the technology cited earlier. Without much delay, the corporation must worry about nationwide mailings, billboards and television advertisements asking consumers whether they have ever suffered harm because of the firm. Remember the mantra "Escalate! Escalate!"

When faced with a lawsuit, the corporation has the option of hiring talented trial lawyers and fighting the case in the courtroom, defending against the claim that its products, services, policies or pricing injured the class of plaintiffs. But will the case be treated fairly? Juries naturally find more sympathy with flesh and blood plaintiffs than with the abstract corporation. Plaintiffs' lawyers may introduce into evidence questionable scientific "research" to buttress a product liability case. No doubt, in a country as large as the United States, they can find an expert to support nearly any far-fetched scientific argument. There are Ph.D. scientists in the United States who believe that unidentified flying objects may be flown by space aliens. It is difficult for jurors and even judges to sort out the junk science from the well-settled science. In any event, it is dangerous for the corporation to take the risk on jurors. In the 1990s, Dow Corning decided to no longer fight the uncertain science related to its breast implants. Instead it filed for bankruptcy in 1995, though its implants have not yet been proved to cause injury (beyond leakage). The authoritative studies of the Mayo Clinic and Harvard could not protect Dow Corning from innumerable rounds of litigation. Even if a corporate defendant wins 100 copycat cases, it cannot prevent another plaintiff from filing case number 101.

The march of junk science continues each day, it seems. In April 2001, a prominent lawyer filed a class action lawsuit against cellular telephone makers on the mere suspicion that these phones might injure users, acknowledging that there is no evidence at this time. A few weeks earlier lawyers filed a class action suit against Colgate-Palmolive, the Walgreen drugstore chain and the American Dental Association. The charge? That the defendants neglected to warn toothpaste users that they might injure their gums by brushing too vigorously. No doubt there are experts on tooth-brushing ready to attack this nearly addictive habit.

With all of these pressures bearing down on a firm, no wonder managers often look at settlement talks like the Godfather's offer you can't refuse. The point here is not to argue against tort actions, nor to argue that corporate defendants are always innocent of wrongdoing. The point is to identify the calculus that tilts the legal system toward more litigation and induces corporations to settle these matters rather than to litigate the merits in a court before a jury.

Some people might wonder, "Why doesn't the corporation fight the case in court? Isn't that the right thing to do? Doesn't principle count anymore?" In fact, corporate executives do not always have the luxury of fighting just to protect truth, justice or their honor. They have a fiduciary responsibility to serve their shareholders. If settling the case reduces the risk to shareholders, the executives may have an obligation to sign on the dotted line. Engaging in a win or die trial may look good in Hollywood, but looks bad on Wall Street. Corporate executives who vainly fight and lose a high stakes case may find themselves personally liable for breaching their duty to shareholders. The law does not permit them to stand on principle when that can undercut their shareholders.

Hunting for Goodwill and Destroying Brand Value

A company is not simply a collection of desks, chairs, wrenches and computers. One cannot figure out the value of a firm simply by stacking up all of the tools in the warehouse and weighing them or auctioning them off. Of course, people add value. Yet even adding the talent of the labor force or the value of patents and trademarks will not necessarily capture the full value of the enterprise. In a modern economy reputation and brand value play enormous roles. You can look at two all-cotton white shirts. Imagine one is plain, without any markings. Another has a Ralph Lauren Polo logo on it. The thread in the Polo logo may cost only a few cents, but it boosts the value of the shirt by many dollars. When Michael Jordan played for the Chicago Bulls basketball team, replicas of his jersey showing number "23" attracted buyers throughout the world. Reverse those numerals and sew on "32" and the value is probably cut in half. The "brand" Jordan is worth hundreds of millions of dollars, as Nike knows. So, too, does the Tiger Woods brand add to Nike's revenue stream. Accountants try to capture the value of such intangibles in a category they call goodwill. The Nobel Prize-winning economist James Tobin devised a related concept called Q, which tries to explain why the total value of companies traded in the stock market so far surpasses the replacement cost of all of the assets owned by the companies.[7] In some cases, the brand and the reputation of a product may be its most valuable asset. To millions of Americans, Kleenex is not just a variety of facial tissue but the generic term they use for facial tissue. McDonald's spends billions of dollars to ensure that a Big Mac tastes the same whether you eat it in Boise or Boston.

Class action lawsuits often aim their arrows at the heart of a company's brand. By threatening to corrupt a brand, plaintiffs' lawyers can command immediate attention. At the same time, they can damage company shareholders. In 1999 automobile insurance firms suffered in the stock market when a class action lawsuit accused them of conspiring to use inferior parts when repairing cars. Consider the injury to brand reputation for a company like Allstate, which has invested many millions of dollars in the motto "You're in good hands with Allstate." In the 1980s, Audi automobile suffered a devastating loss of value as a result of a class action lawsuit alleging "sudden acceleration syndrome," in which the cars purportedly launched themselves even as the drivers kept their feet on the brakes. After a lengthy study, the National Highway Traffic Safety Administration concluded that the drivers had likely stomped on the accelerator, thinking it was the brake. Nonetheless, it took years for Volkswagen to repair the Audi brand image. According to one estimate the Coke brand is worth $69 billion to the Coca-Cola Company. In 2001, Coca-Cola settled a racial discrimination lawsuit for $192.5 million rather than risk further injury to its reputation as a brand of soda beloved by all peoples of all colors throughout the world.

State v. State

Mississippi is known for many good things: mud pies, magnolia trees and Elvis Presley, for example. And, oh, how those Mississippians can write! William Faulkner, Eudora Welty . . . even Tennessee Williams is really from Mississippi. Too bad the state can't write laws as well as it writes gothic novels. In 2002, the U.S. Chamber of Commerce fingered Mississippi as the home of "jackpot justice" and the worst example of tort lawyers run amok. Mississippi's soil is great for growing magnolia trees but it is even better for growing class action lawsuits. Going by the stream of multimillion-dollar jury verdicts, you'd think every citizen in the state had been poisoned by asbestos, tortured by their

HMO or forced to choke on a chain of cigarettes. The record is so bad that companies and industries, some of which haven't even come under scrutiny, are fleeing the state in dismay. In May 2002, the American College of Obstetricians and Gynecologists denounced Mississippi for driving its practitioners out of business and out of state. Here's hoping no midwives have pockets deep enough to merit a stint in the defendant's chair.

Since 1995, seven separate Mississippi juries have banged the gong for $100+ million verdicts. And while Mississippi's story is in some ways just one more chapter in the ongoing struggle between tort lawyers and business, the state's floundering economy has made more apparent some of the real costs of chronic litigiousness.

In a statistical study I conducted with Robert Hahn of the AEI-Brookings Institution Joint Center on regulatory studies, we found that jackpot justice injures ordinary citizens by impeding economic growth.[8] Frivolous lawsuits might even be considered a luxury good. Back in the late 1990s when GDP was galloping along at a record pace we could afford to be cavalier about such impediments to the economy. But as jobs and growth are tougher to come by now, we have to take their threat more seriously. States like Mississippi assume that businesspeople are both evil and stupid. Somehow they figure that after being sued into virtual bankruptcy and given whiplash in the press, businesses will stick around for more of the same. Fat chance.

Last year Toyota weighed the choice of building a new plant in Texas or Mississippi. A letter from Toyota's senior vice president stated that while the Magnolia State was desirable for its pool of skilled labor, infrastructure and quality of life, the "litigation climate in Mississippi is unfavorable, and negatively impacts the state's business climate." [9] The outcry from the Toyota letter finally spurred the state legislature to act, and in June 2004 Governor Haley Barbour signed a far-reaching litigation reform bill.

Yogi Berra said you can sometimes see a lot just by looking. A glance at a recent Harris Poll surveying senior litigators at public corporations asked corporate America to rank the states on issues such as tort and contract litigation, discovery procedures, judges' impartiality and the like. Among the lowest ranking states were Mississippi, West Virginia, Alabama and Louisiana.

Not every southern state performed badly. Virginia grabbed the number-two slot (after Delaware), and Georgia made the top half. Other top-scoring states were scattered around the map, including Washington, Kansas, Connecticut, Arizona and Indiana. Now, let's take a look at which states grew slowest during the boom years of 1995–1999, when per capita state growth averaged 14.2 percent. With such a riproaring economy, only nine states bungled their way to single-digit rates. Sure enough, among the infamous nine were Mississippi, West Virginia and Louisiana. Some of the other dogs brooding in the sub-10 percent kennel include Nevada, Montana, Alaska, Hawaii and Wyoming. All of them, with the exception of Wyoming, fell into the bottom quartile on the Harris survey.

The converse applies as well for the most part. Among those states that treated business well, growth was stronger. The top ten states in the Harris survey earned an average 15.72 percent growth score, beating the average and smashing the bottom ten, which managed just 11.63 percent. Roughly speaking, by equipping tort lawyers with lethal legal weapons aimed at businesses, states rob their citizens of one-third of their potential income growth.

In our books, films and television programs, Americans have tended to glorify the plaintiff's lawyer, toiling alone to battle the Goliaths of American corporate industry. Who could not sympathize with Julia Roberts playing Erin Brockovich or be drawn in by the legal thrillers of that superrich Mississippi novelist John Grisham? It is okay to enjoy Julia Roberts or John Grisham, but that is not the way to make policy or to make law.

There are consequences, as the American College of Obstetricians and Gynecologists warned Mississippi in 2002. Remember the scene in *Gone With the Wind* when Prissy says she "don't know nuthin' 'bout birthin' babies"? Soon, she won't be the only one.

Now, in a debate before the Econometric Society, I would have to admit that there are many explanations for a state's growth rate quite apart from the legal structure. That is why businesspeople also throw themselves into civic discussions of education, taxes and infrastructure. Tort reform alone will not suddenly cure the Biloxi blues or turn Picayune into bustling Portland, Oregon. Nonetheless, the statistical evidence suggests that common sense is, well, sensible. If you handcuff businesses and haul them into kangaroo courtrooms, you do not attract as many businesspeople. And you do not create as many jobs, except as kangaroo keepers.

Big Money, Big Waste

The United States is notorious for its litigation. This is not news. But the dollars involved are staggering. Let's put it in perspective. Consider: a key issue in the contentious 2000 presidential campaign was the size of a tax cut. Presidential candidate George Bush had proposed a $1.6 trillion tax cut over ten years. Then Vice President Gore countered with a set of tax cuts totaling $500 billion. Similar numbers have fueled the 2004 election debate. Analysts believe that a fiscal change of that magnitude is large enough to alter the growth rate of the economy, the level of interest rates and the behavior of households and firms. And yet the cost of litigation to the U.S. economy surpasses any controversial tax cut legislation! Tillinghast-Towers Perrin, the management consulting firm that specializes in insurance matters, calculates that in 2002 alone the United States paid more than $233 billion to handle tort matters. As a country we devote about 2.23 percent of our gross domestic product to litigation. Not only does that exceed what other countries spend by a multiple, but it exceeds the combined federal spending on the departments of Education, Energy and Justice! The key difference is that government programs are determined by the deliberate appropriations decisions of elected officials. Whether they are wise or wasteful, those decisions are public and deliberate. In contrast, litigation costs pile up in a combat-mission atmosphere and a lotterylike disposition of tort cases. The United States required a publicized presidential campaign to decide whether to devote 2 percent of GDP to tax cuts, yet we annually permit more than 2 percent of GDP to leak into litigation struggles without much consideration. In our civics textbooks we learn that only Congress can raise taxes. In our courtrooms we learn that lawyers, judges and jurors wield power over similar sums of money.

Despite the large sums spent, legitimate plaintiffs seldom get rich in class action lawsuits. According to Tillinghast-Towers Perrin they collect less than half the dollars spent on litigation.

The larger portion goes to a combination of administrative and legal costs. And because the claimants' lawyers have strong incentives to build up the number in the class, the average settlement fee per plaintiff gets diminished.

The money spent on litigation does not come for free. There is an opportunity cost for each dollar a defendant corporation pays in damages, legal fees and insurance premiums. Will a defendant firm engage in less research and development? Or try to recoup the losses by charging higher prices? Will a corporation cut off and spin a division into bankruptcy, leading to layoffs of employees? These are some of the unavoidable tradeoffs that emerge when we devote so much money to litigation.

Excessive Class Action Litigation Harms Employees as Well as Shareholders

The damage to a corporation goes beyond its shareholders, of course. Employees, too, will suffer in the legal combat. Over the past twenty years, more corporations have offered stock options and stock ownership to employees as part of a compensation package. According to surveys, about 20 percent of American adults own stock in the company for which they work. The bulk of Home Depot's pension program rests on awarding company stock. These programs energize the incentives for employees, tying their financial gains to the success of the company. Naturally, a drop in stock value hurts such employees. But even those workers who do not own shares have a stake in the firm's performance. Obviously, a firm or division bankrupted by litigation will end up laying off workers. During the 1970s and 1980s, lawsuits (not necessarily class actions) nearly wiped out the U.S.

general aviation industry as paid claims for judgments, settlements and defense costs soared from $24 million in 1977 to $210 million in 1985. During that period, the number of aircraft produced dropped by about 90 percent along with a 70 percent drop in jobs.[10]

Remember when the asbestos scare hit? You must be old. Well, old enough to remember the late 1970s when schools and offices began ripping out dangerous ceiling tiles and insulation materials. The ripping out and the ripping off still goes on. Nobel Laureate Joseph Stiglitz, known for his liberal opinions, led a study concluding that at least sixty thousand jobs have been lost as a result of five hundred thousand claims filed against more than a thousand companies.[11] Workers have typically lost between twenty-five thousand dollars and fifty thousand dollars, plus more than eight thousand dollars in their 401(k) plans as eighty companies have slammed shut their office doors and instead opened the door to bankruptcy court. Sixty percent of the money paid goes to lawyers and court costs. Justice David Souter has called the situation an "elephantine mess," as more than three-quarters of the claims come from people with no current illness but the fear of future symptoms. The Big Three automakers face thousands of lawsuits because they used asbestos in brake linings. GM did not make the asbestos or build the brakes themselves but you will pay more for your Chevy Suburban because employees of defunct companies made the brake linings.

A firm wounded by litigation may not be able to afford pay raises or afford to roll out a new product or service. Economists have shown that an employee's wages are ultimately tied to the capital he has to work with. An automobile worker with better tools produces more and can command better compensation. To borrow a phrase from Winston Churchill, the worker says: "Give us the tools, and we will finish the job." A wounded firm can no longer provide these tools and can no longer deliver on its promises to its employees.

Excessive Class Action Litigation Harms Taxpayers and Consumers

Shareholders certainly suffer when class action lawsuits spin out of control. While most Americans care about the financial markets, few are focused on their portfolios twenty-four hours each day. Most see themselves as investors, but they also have other roles to play, for example, as consumers and taxpayers. Unfortunately, class action lawsuits do damage to these roles as well.

Consumers suffer when mass tort claims raise prices and reduce choice

Firms facing litigation claims may be forced to remove products and services from the market. How does this affect consumers? By cutting competition, litigation pushes consumer prices higher. A surge in lawsuits against nursing homes has driven many insurers out of the business, so that they refuse to insure the facilities. Facing fewer competitors, the remaining insurers may have the power to jack up the prices they charge to nursing homes. (Even with the facilities and the consumers' paying higher prices, the premiums may not cover the skyrocketing claims.)

The U.S. vaccine industry has also shrunk, adding to consumer medical costs. Because vaccines trigger side effects in some people, the industry is vulnerable to lawsuits. No surprise, then, that a wave of litigation impelled about half of the vaccine manufacturers to close down over the past thirty years, leaving vaccines for diseases such as measles and polio in the hands of monopolists who may then charge higher prices.[12] It's cheaper and safer to sell Botox made from a bacterium! Vaccine makers and nursing homes are, of course, complex enterprises. But even in simple cases such as commonplace stepladders we see similar results. According to an article in the *American Bar Association Journal,* product liability concerns tack on 20 percent to the cost of a ladder because consumers who fall off ladders routinely sue the manufacturer.[13] As a result, a number of ladder manufacturers have closed their shops.

Consumers also suffer when risk-averse businesses insist that the consumer meet certain eligibility requirements before they sell their products to them. A pharmaceutical company, for example, may require a doctor's prescription in order to help shield it from liability, even though the drug may be gentle enough for over-the-counter use. This kind of discrimination tends to raise prices and frustrate consumer demand.

In the 1980s, GD Searle, a division of the Monsanto Co., withdrew its intrauterine devices (IUD) from the U.S. contraceptive market because it could not justify defending a rash of lawsuits alleging health problems. Even though the Food and Drug Administration still approves of the device and even though it is used widely in Europe and Canada, American consumers do not have similar options to purchase the product in the United States. In a recent parody appearing in *Time* magazine, a writer suggests that Q-Tip manufacturer Unilever should brace itself for a class action lawsuit since it knows that people use Q-Tips with the dangerous intent of sticking it in their ear (which could injure an eardrum).

Like the push-me-pull-you creature in *Dr. Dolittle,* the litigation mess leads to firms pulling products off the shelves, limiting treatments, while at the same time doctors overtreat, overtest and overprescribe to avoid any possible lawsuit. According to one study, about fifty billion dollars per year are spent on "defensive medicine."[14] Doctors know this drives up costs and makes American employees more expensive to hire. But they are covering their posteriors: "You can't sue me because I was so careful I tested you and treated you for everything from postnasal drip to the bubonic plague."

Consumers suffer when class action lawsuits stunt innovation

In theory, a tort case might induce a defendant firm to develop safer designs. In practice, a Brookings Institution study "found little direct or statistical evidence that specific liability verdicts have led to . . . safer products." In fact, when lawsuits scare away companies from certain product lines, they will cut back their research and development. Following the IUD debacles, the American Medical Association reported that the number of U.S. pharmaceutical companies pursuing research in contraception and fertility dropped from thirteen to one. A survey by the Conference Board, a nonprofit research and forecasting organization, reported that about one-third of large firms had decided not to sell new products because of liability fears.[15]

In recent years a greater portion of U.S. economic growth has come from innovation and from newer products. Firms such as IBM state that about three-quarters of their revenues come from products that are less than two years old. Because class action lawsuits spark a decline in innovation, they endanger the vitality of the U.S. economy.

Country v. Country

Perhaps the United States could withstand the lawyers chipping away at jobs, incomes and investments if other countries suffered the same. I don't know whether misery loves company, but I do know that countries cannot afford to squander competitive advantages. They used to say about the old Washington Senators baseball team that they were "first in war, first in peace and last in the American League east." Well, thanks to Washington, D.C.'s inaction on tort reform we are number one for legal costs, spending twice as much a percentage of GDP as our trading partners. Only Italy plays in the same league with roughly 1.7 percent, compared with less than 1 percent in the U.K., France, Japan, Canada and Switzerland.[16] You may say what you like about these countries and, respectively, their weather, success in battle, homogeneity, latitude or price level. But I've never heard these nations accused of being grossly, irresponsibly unfair to innocent, injured people. By spending twice as much on lawyering, we are losing jobs and seldom gaining more than a stack of coupons.

After assessing the evidence, I estimate that our system cuts our job-making potential by about 5 percent. If we junked the miserable system that rewards gambling on junk science and other excesses, the American economy would create a combination of the following: American jobs could pay 3 percent to 4 percent more on average, and/or America would create 3 percent or 4 percent more jobs for its citizens. Lest you feel like sneezing at a 3 percent to 4 percent wage boost, remember that at 4 percent, our standard of living would double every eighteen years, a far faster clip than during the miraculous Industrial Revolution.

Fast Food

A Scene

The overweight baseball fan jumps to his feet in the bleachers of Wrigley Field, screaming for the Chicago Cubs to hold on to their 3–2 lead in the bottom of the ninth inning. He squeezes a Cubs pennant in his left hand while shoving a mustard-smeared hot dog into his mouth with the right. The Dodgers have a runner on first, who is sneaking a big lead off the base. The Cubs' pitcher has thrown three balls and two strikes to the batter, a notorious power hitter. The obese fan holds his breath as the pitcher winds up and fires a blazing fastball. *"Crack!"* The ball flies over the fan's head into the bleachers for a game-winning home run. The fan slumps to his bleacher seat and has a heart attack.

Who should the fan sue? a. The Cubs for breaking his heart? b. The hot dog company for making a fatty food? c. The hot-dog vendor for selling him a fatty food? d. All of the above?

A few years ago these questions might have seemed preposterous. But now scenes better suited for the absurd stories of Kafka snake their way into serious courtroom encounters. While no federal court has yet heard a case on behalf of sulking baseball fans, last year the U.S. District Court for the Southern District of New York responded to a complaint filed against McDonald's by a class of obese customers, alleging among other things that the company acted negligently in selling foods that were high in cholesterol, fat, salt and sugar.[17] In his opinion in the McDonald's case, Judge Robert W. Sweet suggested that the McDonald's suit could "spawn thousands of similar 'McLawsuits' against restaurants." Sure enough, a few days ago, hungry lawyers gathered in Boston to plot their strategy for future obesity litigation, convening panels with titles like "Food Marketing and Supersized Americans."[18] Recent books with titles like *Fat Land* and *Fast Food Nation* promote the view that fast food firms are harming our health and turning us into a people who are forced to shop in the big and tall sections of clothing stores. The *Wall Street Journal* recently reported that "big and tall" has become a six-billion-dollar business in menswear, "representing more than a 10% share of the total men's market."[19]

In a study entitled "Burgers, Fries and Lawyers" I smashed the biggest myth painted by plaintiffs' lawyers: that America was getting too big for its britches because ignorant people were fooled into putting fattening food into their mouths.[20] The data tell a different story: America's obesity epidemic has struck because highly educated people are dunking doughnuts and stuffing their faces while hunched over computer screens. The percentage of obese college-educated women nearly tripled between the early 1970s and the early 1990s. In comparison, the proportion of obese women without high school degrees rose by 58 percent. Among men, the results were similar. Obesity among those without high school degrees climbed by about 53 percent. But obesity among college graduates jumped by 163 percent. If the "blame fast food" hypothesis made sense, these data would be flipped upside down. Yet plaintiffs' lawyers round up stupid-looking people who would be perfect candidates for Jerry Springer's slugfests and drag them into courtrooms, hoping to hit the judicial jackpot.

Conclusion

When lawyers run an aggressive offense, our economy feels forced to play defense. Doctors waste money on defensive medicine, and personnel managers are scared to death even to give job references. A partner in the leading corporate firm of Proskauer Rose LLP tells his clients that "the safest course is to confirm someone works there and the dates of employment. That's it."[21] What kind of legal system tells people not to speak honestly?

For one hundred years a family of family doctors, the brothers Schwieterman, has helped farmers in Ohio fight off colds, fixed broken arms and delivered babies. In September the brothers will deliver their last baby, the great-granddaughter of their great-grandfather. They are hanging up their rubber gloves because insurance premiums have jumped 150 percent in six years, averaging more than $1,300 per delivery. And in one hundred years of practice, the family doctors have never had a lawsuit payout. They are victims of lawsuit mania, however. More important, so are the young families in Mercer County, Ohio, who may not find a capable doctor to help them bring their children into the world.

An old cliché warns that the two things you cannot avoid are death and taxes. That is true. But those are not the only unavoidable things. In a modern economy we cannot avoid the fact that our jobs, income and retirement savings are ultimately tied to the performance of the companies that do business in America. Moreover, we cannot avoid the fact that a surge in class action lawsuits creates new dangers to these companies—regardless of what products or services they sell. These lawsuits add new volatility to an economic climate already riddled with risk and uncertainty. They threaten to divert attention from serving customers and toward serving legal papers. They tell firms to think twice about locating here and to seek safer ground for their hiring.

No one denies that injured plaintiffs should receive just compensation for legitimate injuries. The question is whether the system adequately weighs these claims and whether plaintiffs' lawyers have excessive incentives to exaggerate the claims and to injure the corporate shareholder. For a class action lawyer, someone else's job is a small thing indeed when compared with a private yacht.

Is there another explanation? Maybe we spend 2.33 percent of the GDP, instead of 0.61 percent of the GDP we spent in 1950, because America is a more devious, dangerous place, with bosses who do not care about their workers and manufacturers who do not care about injuring their customers. Only a terribly gullible jury could believe this; but surely there are lawyers willing to step up to the jury box and wildly wave their arms. Fortunately, the data prove them wrong. Between 1933 and 1993, workplace fatalities plunged by 80 percent. Between 1973 and 1993 alone, workplace fatalities dropped 57 percent. Most workplaces today are safer than homes. The lawyers may scream bloody murder, but they've got fewer victims to scream about.

What should we do? First, judges should launch competitive bidding among lawyers for class action cases. Why should one-third contingency fees reign? A free market in legal fees would push down that proportion and thereby dampen the frenzy to escalate, escalate, escalate. Second, we should adopt the "loser pays" rule, requiring the losing party to pay the winner's expenses. Somehow, the U.K., France, Germany, Sweden, Denmark and the Netherlands have survived without the bullying techniques encouraged by our system. When was the last time you heard liberals denounce those societies as hard-hearted and wickedly rigged against the little guy? What happens if a mean-spirited corporation deliberately wastes money in order to try to bankrupt the plaintiff? The judge can always cut back a gold-plated legal bill. Third, courts should promote early alternative dispute resolution, and plaintiffs should not be permitted to cherry-pick county courts in order to find an addled, prejudicial judge or an easily duped jury. Mississippi would do better to farm out its courts to the cast of *Law & Order* than to continue to distort and diminish its economy.

Gore Vidal once said that after age fifty, litigation takes the place of sex. Clearly our society has made room for both. But it's hard to make room for raging litigation and a prosperous workplace. The United States is no longer the workshop of the world. Merchants and employers have many choices of highly developed, sophisticated places in which to hire, build and sell their wares. When searching for their next base of operation, employers might steer clear of a country where music buyers won money from Arista Records when they discovered that Milli Vanilli was lip-synching. We are swiftly heading toward a "lip-synching" economy: going through the motions but producing only a whisper.

SEVEN

Culture and Hollywood's Tin Ear

Breaking Open Opportunities

SpongeBob SquarePants is packing his bags. Viacom's MTV and Nickelodeon units have announced plans to outsource animation work to India, according to the Bombay daily *Financial Express*. The report suggested that some of the work for such animated series as *Rugrats, CatDog* and *SpongeBob SquarePants* will be produced in India. MTV Network's International COO Alex Ferrari told the newspaper: "We are looking at possibilities of sourcing animation work from India for our group of channels. There is a low-cost advantage. Besides, the quality of Indian animation is good."[1] While one might first react by saying, "They can have SpongeBob," we cannot ignore that the goofy character knows how to make money. India's success comes not just in silly kids' cartoons, many of which have already been outsourced to the Philippines and Japan. From 1994 to 1998, India doubled its share of foreign trademark registrations, and the pace apparently continues.[2]

Clearly, foreign countries take our cartoons seriously. We should not brush off the potential for U.S. exports based on intellectual property and branded images, which generate a half trillion dollars' worth of income and five million jobs.[3] In recent years foreign firms have been able to grab more market share in the intellectual property business.

First, U.S. intellectual property companies, in particular Hollywood firms, are not acting aggressively enough to sell customized product to developing countries, in particular India and China. Rather than condemning outsourcing, the United States should be trying to crack open those markets for more products made with U.S. brainpower. A simple example: the United States imports Spanish-language soap operas from Mexico and Peru. Why do we not write, direct and produce Spanish-language soap operas aimed at the Mexican market? Or for the enormous Indian market? Studio heads have shaken our theater seats with Dolby sound, SenseSurround, and THX, but I'm afraid Hollywood has a tin ear.

Second, U.S. trade negotiators have tended to focus more on the tangible kind of firms that deal with cars, steel and bricks and have not succeeded in cracking down on piracy of intellectual property. In 1999 when George Lucas released his "prequel," *Star Wars: Episode 1—The Phantom Menace,* enterprising, audacious and immoral pirates snuck into U.S. theaters with camcorders and filmed illegal copies. Then they shipped the copies to Asia, where their pirated copies flooded the market. The result? Revenues sank far below expectations when *Star Wars* opened in legitimate theaters. The pirating epidemic even became the subject of a *Seinfeld* television episode in which Jerry is coerced into holding a camcorder in a movie theater. Even if you want to scoff at sci-fi flicks, please note that the same piracy phenomenon plagues software, pharmaceutical goods and agricultural innovations. It is, indeed, serious business. In this chapter, I will show that ripping off intellectual property ultimately damages developing countries, even if it wins them a quick buck or yuan in the short run. If we can make progress creating more intellectual exports and fighting piracy, our outsourcing crisis will appear less lethal, just a wave in the tremendous flows that slosh about the global market.

Hollywood's Tin Ear

Our most lucrative national export, cultural items like film, television and music, are missing out on big export opportunities because the entertainment industry is tone deaf to foreign cultures. The Indian film industry, known as Bollywood (as in Bombay's [now called Mumbai] version of Hollywood) has grown by 65 percent in the past two years, based on everything from modest family dramas to international blockbusters like *Monsoon Wedding* and *Bend It Like Beckham*. Today, six hundred thousand Americans make a living in film, but many of the jobs are threatened, not just by the economic obstacles cited in other chapters of this book, but also by the prevalent vulgarity in U.S. cultural exports. This tone deafness is a symptom of a liberal Hollywood mentality that strives to be as edgy as possible while scorning family values as too corny to be respectable. Hollywood has gained an edge and, in doing so, lost its balance.

While the movie industry in the United States has been shutting down more theaters than it opens, foreign theaters are popping up around the globe. What will they watch and where will those films be made?

Before we can point out the opportunities, we need to step back and look at the economics of moviemaking. This might be a short but frustrating discussion because as the eminent screenwriter William Goldman said, "Nobody knows anything." Goldman, who wrote screenplays such as *Marathon Man, All the President's Men,* and *The Princess Bride,* argues that Hollywood producers and studio executives do not have any reliable clues about what creates box office gold versus box office dross. Do big stars help? Do big budgets mean big revenues? No one bothered to see Harrison Ford's 2002 blight *K-19: The Widowmaker,* which lost $70 million. *My Big Fat Greek Wedding,* which came out a few months earlier, cost $5 million, starred no stars, yet pulled in $354 million, for a 3,400 percent return! And, of course, most studio executives thought Mel Gibson was throwing away a fortune on *The Passion of the Christ* rather than making a fortune. A few months before the completion of *Titanic,* Fox studios began to panic about a production budget that was leaking millions, as if it, too, had been gouged by an iceberg. Sleepless over the $200 million budget, Fox executives turned to Paramount and sold them a 40 percent stake for $65 million. Why not spread the risk around the west side of Los Angeles? Then the movie smashed records and Fox realized it had delivered to Paramount an amazing bargain. Not even the insiders knew that Leonardo de Caprio's dancing, Celine Dion's wailing and a sinking ship would pull in nearly $2 billion. In the early days of Hollywood, Herman Mankiewicz (*Citizen Kane, Pride of the Yankees*) urged writer Ben Hecht (*Gunga Din, His Girl Friday*) to move west: "Millions are to be made out here, and your only competition are idiots. Don't let this get around." Word got out, the hordes of would-be Chaplins and Capras showed up, but few have made economic sense of the place.

In many ways, the movie industry resembles the venture capital industry. Most venture capital projects lose money, but those who fund venture capital activity keep their sanity because the 5 percent to 10 percent of projects that actually make money can bring tremendous windfalls. Those who got in on the ground floor of Google and eBay have long forgotten pets.com and DrKoop.com. Likewise in Hollywood the profits come from a very narrow sliver of movies that show up on the silver screen. In 1995, for example, just four movies earned more than 80 percent of the revenue. The other 296 films hardly paid for popcorn. Fewer than one in six stayed on theater screens longer than two weeks. Only 5 percent lasted more than fifteen weeks. No surprise that so many theaters have upgraded to digital marquees so they do not have to change the title letters by hand each day.

What makes a hit? It's easy to say "advertising" for we are bombarded with marketing gimmicks, from flashy television spots to plastic toys given away at Burger King. Certainly the studios open their wallets for promotions. The average film costs sixty million dollars to make and thirty million dollars to hawk. But 90 percent of the time that thirty million dollars does not bring in the crowds—at least not past the opening weekend. Do the opinions of high-profile critics count? Studios have been known to kowtow to friendly critics with junkets, jackets and cool sunglasses, and also to blacklist unfriendly voices. Only one-third of movie reviews turn out negative. Glenn Lovell of the *San Jose Mercury News* claims that Disney declared him persona non grata at its screenings and media events. Why was he punished? He wrote a lukewarm review of *Beauty and the Beast.* Lovell conducted a survey that found that many critics felt similar slaps. Even the original "thumbs-up" team of Gene Siskel and Roger Ebert were tossed off the screening invitation list by 20th Century Fox for badmouthing *Nuns on the Run.* According to a report in the *American Journalism Review,* Columbia Pictures blackballed *Los Angeles Times* writer Jeffrey Wells Pictures in 1993 for a piece he wrote about the dud *Last Action Hero.* The studio threatened to cancel advertising in the *Times* if his name reappeared. The former critic for *Los Angeles* magazine claimed that he was "banned for life" by Warner Bros. for describing Danny DeVito as "a testicle with arms" in his review of *Other People's Money.*[4] Despite all the attention to critics, though, academic studies show that movie critics make very little difference in the final tally of a film.[5] Blacklists can be better explained by fragile egos than hard finance. Hollywood is a lot like high school—but without acne and with credit cards.

Let's solve the mystery now. What does count? You knew it all along—whether the movie is worth a box of popcorn! In the end, the free market works pretty well, better than the forecasts of whiz-kid studio executives. Audiences do not know in advance that they will like, say, *Forrest Gump*—they've never seen anything like it—but by watching the film, they "discover" that they like it. What do they do next? They tell friends. Together the moviegoers prove to be as sophisticated as Einstein. To build a model of this chain of decision making, economists Arthur De Vany and David Walls resorted to the Bose-Einstein statistical model (incidentally, Bose was from Calcutta), more often used by physicists to describe the unpredictable path of particles.[6] Because the odds of your seeing a movie depend partly on the number of your friends, neighbors and countrymen who have seen it, the Bose-Einstein model points to an unequal distribution when the studios count how many people bothered to pay for their movie. So the Holy Grail of moviemaking is not word of critic or money spent, but essentially word of mouth.

Now that we know to follow word of mouth, we must ask two questions: who is speaking? Is Hollywood listening closely enough? Conservative critic Michael Medved decries the vulgarity of Hollywood fare. He says that "conventional wisdom holds that the big studios emphasize such disturbing, edgy R-rated releases precisely because they perform best at the box office."[7] In fact, R-rated films (which make up 65 percent of the projects) do not do as well as the average for G-rated and PG-rated films.[8] We will examine these data in just a moment. But to give you a head start on my view: I will argue that India and China should be more and more attractive destinations for exports of PG- and G-rated movies and that we are missing opportunities because our product mix is too heavily slanted toward brutal sex and violence. In my view, studio executives should be moving in two new directions, each of which would create more jobs in the United States: Tilt the vulgar meter away from R and develop and create video products specifically intended for export. Please note that when I refer to R-rated films, I do not mean culturally significant works such as *Saving Private Ryan* or *Schindler's List,* which require such ratings to protect children from gruesome historical, religious or literary images.

As a parent of three children, I could happily make a moral argument that studio executives ought to feel dirty from making excessively dirty, violent films. But this chapter is not intended to be a sermon. It is easy to read the cogent social commentaries of Medved, William Bennett, George Will and William F. Buckley, Jr. A number of years ago, Buckley told me that liberals were delighted to have nude dancing in restaurants as long as the dancers got paid at least the minimum wage. Conservatives, of course, wanted to protest both the dancing and minimum wage laws.

Wal-Mart now sells a "progressive scan" DVD player that can filter out and seamlessly skip past graphic violence, sex scenes, or the like. Directors seem slow to get the message, though. The editor of *Audioholics* recalls working as a sound editor on *Time-*

cop (starring that classically trained kickboxer Jean-Claude Van Damme), which featured a totally gratuitous sex scene, with a woman writhing in bed, further spiced up by a few curse words that would lock in the R rating. "Take out a few nonessential elements and the movie could have easily been made a PG-13 rating. Apparently, this didn't mesh with director Peter Hyams's vision," the editor says with a tinge of sarcasm.[9] He also recalls a family-owned Utah video store that angered 20th Century Fox when it offered its local customers the opportunity to delete from *Titanic* a gratuitous scene of a topless woman.

Clearly, there is still a big market for smut and violence. In a movie theater we can spend two hours watching people we would never let into our living room. Still, I will focus on what makes economic sense in the year ahead. I believe that the development of India and China will ultimately create more customers for family-friendly than for family-frightful films.

If, on average, G-, PG- and PG-rated films trounce R-rated ones, why does Hollywood insist on making so many? Are executives twisted and stupid? Perhaps, but there is more to Hollywood's numbers than just the averages. If you pick apart the statistics, you learn that very violent and very sexy films have a built-in audience that will see them no matter how terrible the films are.[10] Are you surprised to hear that we have a mass of dependably crude people ready to buy tickets, as long as the movie is stamped with an *R*? Therefore, R-rated films look less risky to the studios. They seldom make big money, but they seldom lose, either. In baseball terms, they resemble a .270 hitter who is reliable enough to stay in the league. PG-rated films are like sluggers who either strike out or blast home runs. As a result, a studio executive sleeps more soundly when he releases a stomach-turning movie.

Is there any hope, then, for family fare if R-rated films reduce risk—and the executive's odds of being fired? Yes. Although PG films appear more risky, somehow G-rated films also look extremely safe. Only about 5 percent of films get a G rating, yet family films have explosive potential, not just at the box office, but especially in the video rental stores. Rentals make up more than half the revenues for such movies. Of *Variety* magazine's All-Time Top 10 Rentals, seven out of ten were G-rated.[11] When you consider the half billion dollars of *Sound of Music* rentals, it's a darn good thing the von Trapps climbed over those Alps. As the proportion of revenues from video continues to climb, we should expect a rebound in family-friendly fare. Further, studios have a better chance of selling merchandise based on a cuddly or wisecracking cartoon than on a hot-headed wife beater from an R-rated flick. *The Lion King* cost $55 million to make and earned a smashing $800 million from ticket sales. Yet the cash registers have rung up more than $3.5 billion in video and merchandise sales. Not bad for a cartoon based on *Hamlet*.

Why G and PG Can Take Charge Abroad

Conventional wisdom says that I am flat wrong; that Hollywood's best chance for export success requires a combination of sex and violence. Why? Because they are universal themes. You don't need a translator to understand a bedroom scene or a punch to the jaw. When Rambo mowed down dozens with his machine gun, teenage boys around the world got a thrill. The bullets spoke for the character, which is probably best since even people from his native New York had trouble understanding Sylvester Stallone's grunts. Many of those same teenage boys would love to sneak into the theater to hear the grunts in *Showgirls*.

I recognize that sex and violence will continue to sell. So why should Hollywood tone down the vulgar meter? Because G and PG movies will start selling better in developing countries like China, India and Mexico. Why? Three reasons:

First, language barriers are collapsing around the world, and English is de rigueur in countries that are outsourcing destinations. Almost by definition, a country cannot be eligible for white-collar outsourcing or call center outsourcing unless it has a huge stable of English-speaking citizens. PG movies tend to offer more plot and characterization than R-rated, and certainly NC-17-rated movies. Movies with more subtle scripts, relying less on action, sex and violence, typically require awkward subtitles or even dubbing when they are shown outside the United States. But as the English language expands its dominance, foreign audiences will no longer require subtitles or dubbing and, therefore, find American PG and PG-13 movies more and more attractive.

Second, countries that shine in outsourcing tend to be more traditional societies with more traditional mores and family structures. In China the Confucian standards of modesty still exert some power over the loins, as does the Catholic Church in Mexico and the conservative Hindu sensibility in India. Quite often government censors reinforce those traditions. In May 2004, China's culture ministry approved Britney Spears's first tour of that country, but literally insisted she keep her pants on. In April 2004, the government's Administration for Radio, Film and Television slapped a series of new regulations on the media to dampen the trend toward racy, violent content. Some of the rules seem downright frivolous, like forbidding television hosts from dyeing their hair. In Fujian Province, hosts of a local version of *Entertainment Tonight* quickly abandoned their dyed blond locks, and one ditched a stuffed mynah bird that used to perch on his shoulder.[12] Other rules appeared more serious, such as those prohibiting violence, murder and horror before 11 P.M. Traditional mores, reinforced by government boards, affect advertising campaigns as well. In Malaysia an Ogilvy & Mather director designed a television ad for Oxy, a pimple ointment. The scene opens with a man sneaking into a grocery store with a stocking on his head. He looks around nervously. Bystanders panic and faint to the floor, fearing a robbery. The intruder points, not to the cash register, but to a tube of Oxy. He throws money at the clerk and frantically runs out of the store. The Malaysian government vetoed the ad, however, stating that the robberylike scene would scare the viewers.[13]

As for India, I would argue that American PG-rated themes are by far the most popular themes already. Why do I use the word "themes"? Because Bollywood routinely remakes American movies with Indian casts and an Indian setting. Everything from Robin Williams's comedy *Mrs. Doubtfire* to Clark Gable's *It Happened One Night* has been "chutneyed" by Bombay filmmakers. You may recall the Tom Hanks/Meg Ryan romance *Sleepless in Seattle,* but millions of Indians saw it as *Akele Hum Akele Tum.* The "chutney" process involves three additional ingredients: sex scenes are toned down; schmaltz is added to draw a tear from the audience; and singing and dancing show up, sometimes without logic.[14] Bollywood is selective, of course. Filmgoers in Calcutta will probably not see Indians running in fear from Godzilla or worrying about a silly ice age in *The Day After Tomorrow.* In other words, the most promising kinds of film exports to India will be more wholesome family films, or adult films whose plot line does not depend on whores, murderers or unnatural natural disasters. Now it is true that the influence of MTV culture has chipped away at traditional mores around the globe. But the chipping has not yet turned into utter destruction or collapse. A mind-bogglingly large audience sits in Asian theaters waiting for Hollywood to come over with less vulgar fare.

A third reason supports my view on export opportunities: Research shows that, like the spread of English, the spread of other American goods and services portends the successful selling of American film and television. In particular, fast food is a leading indicator for movie tickets.[15] In China, "Big Mac" has become a nickname for American fast food (like Kleenex is for facial tissues in the United States). A 2000 survey showed that almost 50 percent of Chinese city dwellers regularly visit a McDonald's or KFC.[16] While McDonald's has closed franchises in the United States, about one hundred per year have been opening in China. Because Ronald McDonald leads the way for Julia Roberts and Brad Pitt, Chinese moviegoers and television watchers are developing appetites for more than just the easily translated grunts and goons of movies that focus strictly on sex and violence.

Preserving and Protecting "Brand America"

There is no guarantee that American cultural goods and services will continue to be "cool," admired or envied. Culture is, after all, strictly discretionary and often just a matter of taste. As other countries develop economically, more of their purchases are based on tastes, not on necessities or gross commodities. Think about U.S. history. During the 1920s, Americans spent half their incomes on food, a necessity. Nor did they have a choice of one hundred different cereals, from Honey Nut Cheerios to Count Chocula. For all but the wealthiest, shoes were shoes, until Keds came along in 1930 introducing a whole new category. Recall Gertrude Stein's "A rose is a rose is a rose." Not anymore. The

American rose industry now gives you a choice of more than eight hundred varieties of roses. The point here is that as people have more choices and make those choices based on changing tastes, U.S. exporters become more vulnerable. Henry Ford famously offered the Model T in every color you could ask for, "as long as it is black." Have you looked at the Competition Orange Mustang that Ford sells today? Consumers the world over are free to choose *and* free to just say no.

What if U.S. economic dominance and product appeal turn out to have been just a fifty-year fad? Tastes do change, after all. "Hey hey, my my, rock 'n' roll can never die," wailed Neil Young in his 1980 song "Out of the Blue and into the Black." Rocker Kurt Cobain quoted the lyric in his suicide note in 1994. But ask today's hip-hopper about rock and he pictures Mick Jagger and Neil Young in the same old-age home as Perry Como wearing a cardigan sweater. Barbie dolls had a nice forty-year worldwide run, along with GI Joes. Have we already lived through and closed the door on the Barbie doll economy? Did the post–World War II *pax Americana* carry with it *product Americana*? Remember, when the United States conquered Germany, German kids could not wait to swing to Glenn Miller and the big bands. American goods were like gold, and Germans would literally walk a mile for a Camel cigarette. Is the thrill gone? Has the admiration turned to resentment?

Since ancient times, national admiration has often turned to envy and resentment. Ancient texts warn people not to be seduced by foreigners, who are typically characterized by immorality and a lack of cleanliness. Don't let that harlot Delilah near your hair, young Samson, says the Bible. But Samson is predated by an even older tale, the Babylonian epic of Gilgamesh. In this epic from 2000 B.C., an evil harlot from a strange land seduces Enkidu, who brings him to the gates of hell. The French and the Brits have admired and despised each other for centuries. The Brits would refer to syphilis as the French disease, and the French would call it the British disease. During a groundbreaking ceremony for the Chunnel in the early 1990s, English protesters shouted at then-French President François Mitterrand, "Froggy go home! Froggy go home!" Meanwhile, British engineers had to assure that rabid French raccoons could not sneak across the Chunnel and infect English varmints.

The reign of R-rated stuff emanating from Hollywood is all the more sad because it diminishes America's image in the world and further fuels resentment. In the 1920s Georges Clemenceau accused the United States of miraculously sliding straight from barbarism to degeneration without passing through civilization. Consider: the American cowboy image used to command respect and romantic fantasies of a simpler life. John Wayne and Jimmy Stewart were noble characters in international commerce. The main character in the 1950s movie *Shane* symbolized the idea of America as a welcome intruder who saved, redeemed and civilized bloody Europe during two world wars. Throughout the Wild West and the western world the poignant last words of *Shane* resounded, as the young boy cries for the departing hero to stay: "Pa's got things for you to do, and Mother wants you . . . Shane, Shane! Come back!" In a tribute to Ronald Reagan, the Polish electrician-turned-liberator Lech Walesa described how his party turned a Hollywood poster into an emblem of liberty. They inserted the red SOLIDARITY banner over Gary Cooper's face in *High Noon,* a movie in which Cooper plays a sheriff fighting for justice: "Cowboys in Western clothes had become a powerful symbol for Poles. Cowboys fight for justice. Fight against evil, and fight for freedom," he wrote.[17]

But what have we done to the American image in the past few decades? The cowboy no longer looks like the savior and redeemer. Today, Europeans typically insult President Bush by calling him a "cowboy"—wild, barbaric and interested only in his own piece of the pie. Their accusation may be reckless, but we must worry about the status of our symbols. Rather than fighting for liberty and justice, Hollywood has treated us to cynical vigilantes. The despair and malaise of the 1970s brought us Charles Bronson in *Death Wish* and Robert De Niro as the unforgettable, maniacal Travis Bickle in *Taxi Driver.* For every uplifting Stephen Spielberg or Tom Hanks film celebrating noble soldiers, astronaut explorers or extraterrestrials, we get a dozen senseless rape and murder stories.

The point is this: developing countries—those most likely to benefit from outsourcing—are waiting to watch the best that America has to offer in the moving image. By making and selling drivel, studio executives might turn a quick buck. But ultimately they undermine the American brand and, therefore, their own ability to make money. I would appeal to their wallets, not just their consciences, for we can be sure they do care about the former.

Beyond Americana

Though the American brand commanded respect throughout the world, that image was often developed and enhanced by people who started elsewhere. Frank Capra, director of *It's a Wonderful Life,* started in Palermo, Sicily. Billy Wilder, who directed the brilliant drama *Sunset Boulevard* and the classic comedy *Some Like It Hot,* escaped from Nazi Germany. And, of course, that most American of comics, Bob Hope, began life as Leslie

Townes Hope in Eltham, England. More recently, Hollywood has fallen for a string of Australian heartthrobs like Russell Crowe, Hugh Jackman and Nicole Kidman. For the most part Hollywood has taken foreign talent and squeezed them into American costumes and accents. Instead of trying to homogenize foreign talent, studios should also consider channeling their talent to the billions of people who live outside our borders. Warner Bros. signed up the young Mexican director Alfonso Cuaron to direct *Harry Potter and the Prisoner of Azkaban.* Cuaron had directed the stunning (and, yes, racy) *Y Tu Mama También* (*And Your Mother Too*). His Harry Potter movie is making hundreds of millions for Warner Bros. A smart move. But why not also hire the prodigy to direct a movie aimed at the billions of Hispanics who live in the United States and throughout Latin America?

As Chinese, Latin American and Asian countries become more wealthy (partly through U.S. outsourcing!), they will also become a more vibrant export destination for entertainment. The U.S. entertainment industry should be deploying its know-how to produce movies and television shows for foreign markets. Twenty years ago when there was no middle class in China, that might not have made sense. Now China has more wireless telephones than the United States and more than two hundred million people who qualify as middle class. Similar stories emerge in India, Brazil and Mexico. The United States has the resources and the know-how to penetrate those markets, just as Mexican producers have triumphed by selling soap operas to U.S. television stations. A few years ago, store owners in Spain changed their hours in order to avoid conflict with a Mexican soap. A Mexican *telenova* (a story adapted for television) swept to first place in South Korea with such force that many Korean viewers apparently thought the show originated in Seoul. Turkish viewers drove to the top of the ratings a Mexican show called *Los Ricos También Lloran (The Rich Also Cry).* For the most part, major Hollywood studios today resign themselves simply to earning revenues on the movies and shows that they make for the American audience. But they should be getting in the business of producing specifically for export, too, and for American ethnic groups that prefer stories aimed at Chinese, Hispanic and Indian audiences. If a small nation like Peru can export a drama like *Luciana y Nicolas* both to St. Petersburg, Florida, and St. Petersburg, Russia, then so can Paramount and MGM. The United States has as many Hispanics as Peru, after all. While U.S. media firms like Univisión and Telemundo do cater to American Hispanics, their export reach is more modest. The people who get those jobs outsourced from the United States now have incomes and certainly enough spare change to pay for a good night out. Who will provide it?

Now, Hollywood faces another crisis, which results from union rules that drive up production costs. Canada, Australia and the Czech Republic have grabbed market share from the United States by offering tax breaks and less onerous union rules. Though I have no interest in seeing the film *Kill Bill Vol. 1,* I can report that director Quentin Tarantino shot much of the footage in Beijing, including a blood-soaked scene in a Tokyo restaurant. Many of the sequel's scenes were filmed in Mexico, including one "shot in a real Mexican brothel, a tattered shack with makeshift tables, and real whores lying in hammocks." A literature teacher at MIT commented that "Tarantino [probably] did not pay these women union wages."[18]

Even if union requirements make the actual shooting of films less profitable in Los Angeles, U.S.-based producers, writers, directors, marketers and other professionals can still earn incomes. Critics of globalization call it the hollowing out of America. In

Japan they called it the doughnut economy, when assembly jobs skipped across the sea to China. I would urge the United States to adopt what I call the jelly doughnut strategy. What's that? The jelly doughnut strategy understands that some jobs will go to places where labor costs are cheaper. Yet it insists on fighting for the most valuable jobs—those that depend on creativity and brainpower. They make up the sweet jelly center of the economy; for example, the designers of new products and the researchers of new medicines. In colloquial terms, the creative "brains behind the operation." In Hollywood, that means the producers, directors, writers, editors and wizards of special effects. It does not necessarily mean the guy holding the cue cards or the boom microphone. Think about sports for a moment, in particular the Wimbledon tennis tournament. British tennis players hardly ever win the trophy. Nonetheless, England sure squeezes buckets of money from the event through tourism, admissions tickets and sporting gear bearing the "W" logo. The jelly doughnut strategy tells Hollywood to compete more aggressively in the international market, even if not every frame of film gets shot on a back lot in Burbank.

The Left Abroad

The U.S. entertainment industry faces two other challenges beyond Hollywood's tin ear and figuring out how to surmount union demands for wages and overtime. These challenges can be blamed on left-wing thinking overseas. The first is piracy, the other cultural protectionism. Let's take just a few minutes to understand these international plagues, which also cost us jobs and money. The French Socialist Pierre Proudhon said, "Property is theft!" The remaining left-wingers in China and India feel little guilt over permitting their citizens to steal our copyrighted, patented and trademarked material. I call it brain theft. If you watch *Lord of the Rings* in China, there is a 90 percent chance that someone stole it without paying a fee to the talent who created the film. If you are running a spreadsheet in India, the odds are nearly 70 percent that someone ripped off a copyright holder.[19] About twenty billion dollars leak out of U.S. pockets from such theft. Considering all the thievery, it's a wonder that the U.S. economy still sells so much abroad. Though you often hear politicians and pundits bemoaning the U.S. trade deficit, please note that the United States piles up a twenty-billion-dollar surplus in patent licenses and other technology designs and models. In other words, our "bread and butter" come from ideas. Piracy means that people in other countries are illegally eating our lunch. Communist Chinese bureaucrats sometimes defend brain theft by appealing to Confucius (who never got a royalty from a fortune cookie). Confucian philosophy exalted copying, memorizing and imitating as a "noble art," a way to honor ancestors. According to this thinking, Chinese people earned more respect for preserving and spreading history, rather than creating something new. A noted work on this topic is entitled *To Steal a Book Is an Elegant Offense.* Even Confucius himself claimed that he was simply transmitting what he had been taught, rather than making anything up on his own.[20] I suppose originality is the art of concealing your sources. Countries that benefit from U.S. outsourcing must understand that they face a terrible political backlash if they do not more vigorously fight brain theft.

In addition to rampant piracy, the United States should also be busting down the walls of cultural protectionism. For example, the French limit the market share of American television programs to 40 percent, granting "affirmative action" to their own.

Never mind that the world's biggest entertainment companies include Sony of Japan and Bertelsmann of Germany. Likewise, China won't let American cartoons exceed 40 percent. Why not let the people decide? In 1993 French Minister of National Education and Culture Jack Lang poured millions of francs and substantial government prestige into *Germinal,* a movie based on a classic Émile Zola story about the monotonous life of striking coal miners. The producers attracted international headliner Gérard Depardieu to star in the film about the 1860s. What better way for Socialists to arouse French patriotism? Unfortunately, at the weekend opening, French moviegoers raced right past the sooty coal miners to grab their seats for a movie about dinosaurs, something called *Jurassic Park.* T. rex beat J. Lang at the box office. *Sacre bleu!* India, Malaysia and South Korea also limit American films, with the Korean government insisting that domestic movies dominate at least 106 days per year. Does affirmative action for media make sense anymore, in a world with thousands of television stations and billions of Web sites? In July 2004, David Beckham's half-naked body stretched across the cover of *Vanity Fair:* a British guy idolized in an Indian movie, now playing soccer for a Spanish team. A few weeks earlier, my wife took my daughters to the rousing international sensation *Mamma Mia:* an English girl and mum live on a Greek Island, singing a Swedish band's tunes, with a title song named after an Italian exclamation. *Mama mia,* do 1.1 billion Indians and 1.3 billion Chinese really need affirmative action?

I raise these issues of piracy and cultural affirmative action to show that the United States is not alone in battling loony policies, which claim to protect people but instead prevent them from living freer, more prosperous lives.

EIGHT

Conclusion

The Battle Against Friendly Fire

Grizzled military men jest that the only thing more accurate than enemy fire is friendly fire. Amicide, death by accidental friendly fire, is the embarrassing secret of warfare. It is only slightly less embarrassing when a solider merely shoots off his own toe and hobbles back Stateside, with nosy neighbors asking, Where is your Purple Heart? In this book I have tried to show that our most fearsome economic enemies are not the hardworking, striving young people of China, Asia, Eastern Europe or Latin America. Nor are they the U.S. CEOs angling to eke out profits and pay bigger dividends to shareholders and bigger bonuses to employees. We are not suffering from enemy fire at all. Instead we are crippled by friendly fire: rules, regulations and taxes that knock down the chances of our young people's succeeding in future decades. Those bullets are all etched "Made in USA."

Left-wing politicians and pundits refuse to confront the dangerous debacles in education, entitlements, litigation and immigration. They focus instead on the threat of outsourcing. Like a flock of Chicken Littles, they stay busy chewing on their claws, worrying that outsourcing will drain millions of jobs from our economy. In the previous chapters, I have shown that our own policies cost our economy about two trillion dollars. The reforms I urge would help create more than 16 million jobs, enough to stanch the outsourcing wave into a gentle ripple.[1] Do those numbers sound too high, too optimistic? Is it so hard to imagine your friends, neighbors and countrymen performing their work 10 percent to 20 percent better or more efficiently? If you cannot imagine it, I suggest pulling the plug on their televisions, because they spend one-quarter of their waking hours staring at it.[2] Surely, there is room for our economy to improve and grow.

How did we get in this mess? Over the past forty years, our government has tried to coddle us and protect us from, well, life. If we shake up the education system, we might dent the pride or self-esteem of some teachers. So the unions say no to reforms that could create a smarter workforce and 1 million jobs. If we redesign the Social Security and Medicare systems, some thirty-year-old dullard may walk around in a stupor for the next forty years and forget to save for his own retirement. So instead we must do nothing and let the systems career toward a crash. Never mind that we could create more than eight million jobs if we had the nerve. If we revamp the tort system, why the next chap who spills hot coffee on his pants may not be able to sue. Surely, every pimple, pockmark and stain deserves a lawsuit. So the legal system frightens businesses from opening up or hiring Americans, and we lose nearly 2 million jobs. If we fight the ludicrous epidemic of occupational licensing, some unqualified person might actually start a florist shop and stick a wilted red rose in a vase next to an orange geranium. Or a dentist in Cleveland might drop the price for a tooth cleaning because his former hygienist has set up shop down the road. Excessive licensing and wrongful termination worries cost us 4.5 million jobs. If we reinvent our immigration program, we might dare to invite in a smart doctor who could help cure breast cancer, rather than an old gravedigger who really doesn't have the strength to pick up a shovel anymore.

Here's what happened to the United States and what has sparked the outsourcing fears: Since the 1960s, each year we've lost a little nerve, gained another bureaucrat, another lawyer, another layer of protection against life's uncertainties. We have gotten used to a government that aims to coddle us but ends up both preventing us from growing and dampening the innate American spirit. The spirit still stirs but gets buried under the weight of the nanny state. I'm all for seatbelts and I have nothing against fluoridated water, but I wonder whether we are going too far. A child reaches for an eight-ounce glass of whole milk, and her mother rushes to stop her. It could raise her cholesterol. Put down that lollypop or you'll get diabetes in sixty years! A few months ago I made the mistake of bringing a few six-packs of yogurt to my daughter's end-of-school party. I didn't notice that the yogurt used aspartame as a sweetener. You'd think I was Dr. Jekyll trying to pour an evil potion down their throats. We might as well clothe ourselves in bubble wrap and hire food testers from the Secret Service. Were Americans always so jittery? When I was a kid, we played in a sandbox. I don't know where the sand came from, but I doubt my parents lugged bags of sterilized sand from Toys R Us. Ironically, some doctors now think that peanut allergies might be traced to kids' not ingesting enough germs!

Americans have been so trained to look for government help that when outsourcing stories break into the headlines, politicians immediately race to the microphone to stop the scourge. But how? By locking the doors to trade? By taxing firms even more and thereby guaranteeing that they will hire fewer Americans? By trying to lock in place the standard of living of 2004 before white-collar outsourcing smashes onto our shores like a tidal wave? It's a good thing Teddy Roosevelt did not lock us into the standard of living of 1904 or we would never drive cars, fly on airplanes or expect to live past the age of fifty. Without the progress of the twentieth century, Milton Berle said we'd all be watching television by candlelight. (Of course, postal delivery would be no different.)

In truth, you cannot freeze history. Whenever I have traveled to the former Soviet Union, I have been struck by the decrepit state of grand cities like Odessa and St. Petersburg, where chipped stones and cratered foundations plague gorgeous baroque buildings. At the Odessa Opera and Ballet Theater, sculptures of mythic beasts, panthers and chariots greet you, along with a ceiling exquisitely painted with scenes from *Hamlet* and *A Midsummer's Night Dream.* In St. Petersburg, go to the Hermitage, the former Winter Palace of the czars, and admire the masterpieces of Leonardo da Vinci and Raphael displayed in a rococo dream world of columns and statuary. But the crumbling stones depressed me, as St. Petersburg's acrid summer air flowed through open windows to degrade and decay the paintings. Then it struck me: The problem with socialism was not that it could not keep up with twentieth-century capitalism—it could not even keep up with the standard of living of 1917!

American government officials today cannot put our standard of living in a lockbox to preserve, protect and defend us. Franklin D. Roosevelt warned us of fearing fear itself; now we fear *life* itself. If we try to stay in place, as the Soviets tried, we will inevitably slip backward. The physicists call it entropy. Jimmy Carter called it malaise. He sat in front of a fire and spoke to us in a cardigan. His message of caution and worry was so dull and depressing the fire almost went out. As countries grow older, they get encrusted with the barnacles of special interest groups that latch on and won't let go.[3] They must be cracked open and broken off. Perhaps outsourcing will spur us to pick up and start swinging the chisels and picks left over from the toppling of the Berlin Wall.

To paraphrase Churchill, Americans did not sail the perilous Atlantic, scale the Appalachians and struggle past the Rockies because we were made of cotton candy. Though that would be a sweet dessert to celebrate millions of new jobs.

Notes

ONE. What Are We Facing?

1. John Hagel III, "Offshoring Goes on the Offensive," *McKinsey Quarterly,* no. 2 (2004), p. 24.
2. Reuven Brenner, *The Force of Finance* (New York: Textere, 2001), p. 29.
3. Marquis James and Bessie R. James, *The Story of Bank of America* (New York: Beard Books, 2002).
4. Stephen Siwek, *Copyright Industries in the U.S.: 2002 Report* (Washington, DC: International Intellectual Property Alliance, 2002).
5. Norihiko Shirouzu, "Big Three's Outsourcing Plan: Make Part Suppliers Do It," *Wall Street Journal,* June 10, 2004, p. A1.
6. Americans are also free to invest in the shares of companies that outsource in order to boost profits. One study has shown that aggressive outsourcers achieve stronger stock appreciation. See Kerry A. Dolan with David Whelan, "The Great Offshore Wimp Out," *Forbes,* April 26, 2004, p. 48.
7. Ashok Deo Bardhan and Cynthia A. Kroll, "The New Wave of Outsourcing," Fisher Center for Real Estate and Urban Economics, University of California, Berkeley, Fall 2003.
8. Ryan Chittum, "Rise in Offshore Jobs Expected," *Wall Street Journal,* May 5, 2004, p. B6.
9. Ray A. Smith and Alex Frangos, "Outsourcing Likely to Slow Office Rebound," *Wall Street Journal,* June 2, 2004, p. B4.

10. Matthew Slaughter, "Multinational Corporations, Outsourcing and American Wage Divergence," National Bureau of Economic Research Working Paper 5253 (1995). Interestingly, Slaughter is coauthor of a study suggesting that globalization creates economic insecurity. See Kenneth F. Scheve and Matthew J. Slaughter, "Economic Insecurity and the Globalization of Production," National Bureau of Economic Research Working Paper W9339 (November 2002).

11. See Hagel, p. 22.

12. IMA, "Why Barbados?" April 15, 2004 presentation.

TWO. Silicon, Soy and Curry

1. *New York Times,* August 24, 1964, p. 26.

2. U.S. Senate Subcommittee on Immigration and Naturalization of the Committee on the Judiciary, Washington, D.C., February 10, 1965, pp. 1–3.

3. For contrasting views, see George J. Borjas, "The Economics of Immigration," *Journal of Economic Literature,* December 1994, pp. 1667–717 and Michael E. Fix, Jeffrey S. Passell, *Immigration and Immigrants: Setting the Record Straight* (Washington, D.C.: Urban Institute, 1994).

4. National Research Council; (check www.prcdc.org/programs/immigration/immigration.html.)

5. Walter A. Ewing, "A Study in Distortion," American Immigration Law Foundation (2003), p. 2.

6. Testimony of Elizabeth C. Dickson before the Senate Committee on the Judiciary, September 16, 2003.

7. "High Tech Workers Become a New Focus of Immigration Debate," Stanford University News Service, October 22, 1996.

8. Randall E. Stross, "Microsoft's Big Advantage—Hiring Only the Supersmart," *Fortune,* November 25, 1996, p. 14.

9. See William J. Broad, "U.S. Is Losing Its Dominance in the Sciences," *New York Times,* May 3, 2004, p. A19.

10. AnnaLee Saxenian, *Local and Global Networks of Immigrant Professionals in Silicon Valley* (San Francisco: Public Policy Institute of California, 2002).

11. Madeline Zavodny, "The H-1B Program and Its Effect on Information Technology Workers," *Federal Reserve Bank of Atlanta Economic Review,* Third Quarter, vol. 88, no. 3.

12. See James Rauch, "Ethnic Chinese Networks in International Trade," *Review of Economics and Statistics* 84:1 (February 2002); Keith Head, John Ries and Donald Wagner, "Immigrants as Trade Catalysts," in A. E. Safarian and Wendy Dobson, eds., *The People Link: Human Resource and Linkages across the Pacific* (Toronto: University of Toronto Press, 1997); and Joel Kotkin, *Tribes* (New York: Random House, 1992).

13. David Card, "Immigrant Inflows, Native Outflows, and the Local Labor Market Impacts of Higher Immigration," *Journal of Labor Economics,* vol. 19, issue 1, 2001; Robert W. Fairlie and Bruce D. Meyer, "Does Immigration Hurt African-American Self-Employment?" National Bureau of Economic Research Working Paper W6265 (November 1997).

14. John Doherty, "No Irish Need Apply," *Boston Magazine* (March 2002).

15. See Jean-Baptiste Meyer and Mercy Brown, "Scientific Diasporas: A New Approach to the Brain Drain" prepared for the World Conference on Science, UNESCO (July 1999) and Michel Beine, Frederic Docquier and Hillel Rapoport, "Brain Drain and LDC's: Winners and Losers," Institute for the Study of Labor, Discussion Paper 819.

16. Ulrich Eberl, "A High Tech Laboratory Called Israel," Siemens Webzine (January 1999).

17. Mark Twain, *The Innocents Abroad,* Chapter LVI.

18. www.cic.gc.ca/english/skilled.

19. Government of Canada, Advisory Council on Science and Technology, "Stepping Up," (March 25, 2003).

THREE. Education

1. Darius Lakdawalla, "The Declining Quality of Teachers," National Bureau of Economic Research Working Paper 8263 (April 2001).

2. Claudia Goldin, "The Human-Capital Century and American Leadership: Virtues of the Past," *Journal of Economic History* 61 (2): pp. 263–92.

3. Claudia Goldin and Lawrence Katz, "Education and Income in the Early 20th Century: Evidence from the Prairies," *Journal of Economic History* 60 (3): pp. 782–818.

4. Dale W. Jorgenson, Mun S. Hoh and Kevin J. Stiroh, "Information Technology, Education, and the Sources of Economic Growth Across U.S. Industries," Harvard University Working Paper (April 2002); Stephen D. Oliner and Daniel E. Sichel, "The Resurgence of Growth in the Late

1990s: Is Information Technology the Story?" Federal Reserve Board Working Paper (May 2000).

5. See Eric A. Hanushek and Dennis D. Kimko, "Schooling, Labor-Force Quality, and the Growth of Nations," *American Economic Review* 90 (5): pp. 1184–208; Jess Benhabib and Mark M. Spiegel, "The Role of Human Capital in Economic Development: Evidence from Aggregate Cross Country Data," *Journal of Monetary Economics* 34 (2): pp. 143–73; and Robert J. Barro and Jong-Wha Lee, "International Data on Educational Attainment: Updates and Implications," National Bureau of Economic Research Working Paper 7911 (September 2000).

6. Yolanda K. Kodrzycki, "Educational Attainment as a Constraint on Economic Growth and Social Progress," Federal Reserve Bank of Boston 47th Economic Conference Proceedings (December 2002), pp. 42–43.

7. *Brown Center Report on American Education* (Washington: Brookings Institution, 2003).

8. Discounting to age eighteen, and ninety-four thousand dollars discounting to age nine at a 6 percent interest rate. Derek Neal and William Johnson, "The Role of Premarket Factors in Black-White Wage Differentials," *Journal of Political Economy* 104 (5): pp. 869–95; lower, but still impressive estimates are cited in Richard J. Murnane, John B. Willett and Frank Levy, "The Growing Importance of Cognitive Skills in Wage Determination," *Review of Economics and Statistics* 77 (2): pp. 251–66.

9. Murnane, Willett and Levy, op. cit.

10. Eric A. Hanushek and Steven G. Rivkin, "Understanding the 20th Century Growth in U.S. School Spending," National Bureau of Economic Research Working Paper W5547 (April 1996).

11. Marigee Bacolod, "The Role of Alternative Opportunities in the Female Labor Market in Teacher Supply and Quality: 1940–1990," (UCLA Department of Economics, 2001).

12. *Brown Center Report on American Education* (Washington: Brookings Institution, 2003) and Ron Zimmer, *Charter School Operations and Performance: Evidence from California* (Santa Monica: Rand Education, 2003).

13. Caroline Hoxby, "School Choice and School Productivity," National Bureau of Economic Research Working Paper 8873 (April 2002) and Eric A. Hanushek and Steve G. Rivkin, "Does Public School Competition Affect Teacher Quality," in Caroline Minter Hoxby, ed., *The Economics of School Choice* (Chicago: University of Chicago Press, 2003), pp. 23–47.

14. Survey from Heritage Foundation (Washington, D.C., July 2003).

15. See Frederick Hess, "Without Competition, School Choice Is Not Enough," American Enterprise Institute Online (May 1, 2004).

16. Todd G. Buchholz, *New Ideas from Dead Economists* (New York: Plume, 1999).

17. Diana Jean Schemo, "When Students' Gains Help Teachers' Bottom Line," *New York Times,* May 9, 2004, p. 1.

FOUR. The Taxman Cometh and Taketh

1. "A Philadelphia Report Card," Federal Reserve Bank of Philadelphia (January 2001), p. 17.

2. See Louis T. Wells, "Investment Incentives: An Unnecessary Debate," *The CTC Reporter,* United Nations Center on Transnational Corporations (Autumn 1986) and S. Guisinger, et al., *Investment Incentives and Performance Requirements* (New York: Praeger, 1985).

3. Kevin M. Murphy and Finis Welch, "Perspectives on the Social Security Crisis and Proposed Solutions," *American Economic Review* 88 (May 1998), p. 142.

4. See Todd G. Buchholz, *Safe at Home* (Washington, D.C.: Homeownership Alliance, 2002) and Susan Cohen, "Generation Next," *Washington Post Magazine,* June 1, 1997, p. 8.

5. Laurence J. Kotlikoff and Scott Burns, *The Coming Generational Storm* (Cambridge, MA: MIT Press, 2004), p. xv. Also see my review in the *Wall Street Journal,* "Tempest in the Tax Code," April 21, 2004.

6. James Brooke, "Tough Sell: Japanese Social Security," *New York Times,* May 6, 2004, p. W1.

7. Kotlikoff and Burns, op. cit., p. 145.

8. Constantijn W. A. Paanis and Lee A. Lillard, "Socioeconomic Differentials in the Returns of Social Security" (Santa Monica, CA: Rand, 1996).

9. www.pef.org/special_postings/dolcalltoaction.htm.

10. Testimony of Daniel M. Steen before the House Ways and Means Committee, March 12, 2003.

11. Michael D. Hurd, review of *Economics of Population of Aging* by James Schulz, et al., in *Journal of Economic Literature* (September 1992), p. 1530; David M. Cutler, Mark McClellan and Joseph Newhouse, "What

Has Increased Medical Spending Bought?" *American Economic Review* 88 (May 1998), p. 132.

12. Dora Costa, *The Evolution of Retirement: An American Economic History, 1880–1990* (Chicago: University of Chicago Press, 1998), pp. 7–10; Jonathan Gruber and David Wise, "Social Security and Retirement: An International Comparison," *American Economic Review* 88 (May 1998), pp. 159–60.

13. Cohen, op. cit., p. 8.

14. Joseph P. Newhouse, *Free for All: Lessons from the RAND Health Insurance Experiment* (Cambridge: Harvard University Press, 1993); Matthew J. Eichner, "The Demand for Medical Care: What People Pay Does Matter," *American Economic Review* 88 (May 1998); Jonathan Skinner and John E. Wenberg, "How Much Is Enough? Efficiency and Medical Spending in the Last Six Months of Life," National Bureau of Economic Research Working Paper 6513 (April 1998).

15. See David M. Cutler and Brigitte C. Madrian, "Labor Market Responses to Rising Health Insurance Costs: Evidence on Hours Worked," National Bureau of Economic Research Working Paper 25525 (April 1996).

16. Laura M. Litvan, "Generation X's Social Security," *Investor's Business Daily* (March 25, 1997), p. 1 and Meredith Bagby, *Rational Exuberance* (New York: Dutton, 1998), pp. 60, 81.

17. Paul Samuelson, one of the greatest among liberal Nobel Laureate economists, made this point when the baby boomers were toddlers. Few listened. Paul A. Samuelson, "An Exact Consumption Loan Model of Interest with or Without the Social Contrivance of Money," *Journal of Political Economy* 66 (December 1958), pp. 467–82.

18. *Chicago Tribune,* August 18, 1989, quoted in Kotlikoff and Burns, p. 129.

19. G. Reuber, et al., "Private Foreign Investment in Development," Clarendon Press for the OECD Development Centre, Oxford, 1973.

20. KPMG Corporate Tax Rate Survey, January 2004.

21. John D. McKinnon, "U.S. Overseas Tax Is Blasted," *Wall Street Journal,* May 5, 2004, p. A4.

FIVE. Barriers to Entry

1. Linda Lee, *The Bruce Lee Story* (Santa Clarita, CA: Ohara Publications, 1989) and James Bishop, *Remembering Bruce Lee* (Los Angeles: Cyclone

Books, 1999). Ironically, Lee was not satisfied with his performance and wondered why the fight took so long.

2. See Todd G. Buchholz, *New Ideas from Dead Economists* (New York: Plume, 1999), p. 35.

3. George J. Stigler, "The Theory of Economic Regulation," in *The Bell Journal of Economics and Management Science,* vol. II (Spring 1971), pp. 3–21.

4. Laurie Roberts, "State Rushes in Where Outlaws Dare to Braid," *Arizona Republic,* March 17, 2004. Following a lawsuit by the Institute of Justice and many media stories detailing the outrage, the Arizona legislature stepped in and adjusted the law to let Essence off the hook.

5. Milton Friedman and Simon Kuznets, *Income from Independent Professional Practice* (New York: National Bureau of Economic Research, 1945); Marc T. Law and Sukkoo Kim, "Specialization and Regulation: The Rise of Professionals and the Emergence of Occupational Licensing Regulation" (Washington, D.C.: Institute for Justice, April 2004, p. 5).

6. William Mellor, *Is New York City Killing Entrepreneurship?* (Washington, D.C.: Institute for Justice, 1996).

7. Morris M. Kleiner, "Occupational Licensing," *Journal of Economic Perspectives,* vol. 14, no. 4 (Fall 2000), p. 191.

8. Ibid., p.199.

9. See Simon Rottenberg, ed., *Occupational Licensure and Regulation* (Washington, D.C.: American Enterprise Institute, 1980).

10. Charles J. Wheelan, *Politics or Public Interest? An Empirical Examination of the Political Economy of Occupational Licensure* (Chicago: University of Chicago manuscript, 1998).

11. Simeon Djankov, Rafael La Porta, Florencio Lopez-de-Silane and Andrei Shleifer, "The Regulation of Entry," *Quarterly Journal of Economics,* vol. 117, issue 1, 2002, pp. 1–37 and ——— and Juan Botero, "The Regulation of Labor," National Bureau of Economic Research Working Paper W9756 (June 2003).

12. Tom Rademacher, cited by Kleiner, "Don't Try This at Home!" *Ann Arbor News,* February 9, 1997, p. A-11.

13. Alia Beard Rau, "Teen Earns, Learns as He Fights Roof Rats," *Arizona Republic,* February 23, 2004.

14. Morris M. Kleiner, Robert S. Gay and Karen Greene, "Barriers to Legal Migration: The Case of Occupational Licensing," *Industrial Relations,* vol. 21, no. 3, pp. 383–91.

15. Marianne Bertrand and Francis Kramarz, "Does Entry Regulation Hinder Job Creation? Evidence from the French Retail Industry," (German) Institute for the Study of Labor, Discussion Paper 415 (January 2002).

16. Lawrence Shepard, "Licensing Restrictions and the Cost of Dental Care," *Journal of Law and Economics,* vol. 21, no. 1 (1978), pp. 187–201; Morris M. Kleiner and Robert T. Kudrle, "Does Regulation Affect Economic Outcomes? The Case of Dentistry," *Journal of Law and Economics,* vol. 43, no. 2 (2000), pp. 547–82; Sidney L. Carroll and Robert J. Gaston, "Occupational Restrictions and the Quality of Service Received: Some Evidence," *Southern Economic Journal,* vol. 47, no. 4 (1981), pp. 959–76; Robert G. Evans, "Professionals and the Production Function," S. Rittenberg, ed., in *Occupational Licensure Regulation* (Washington, D.C.: American Enterprise Institute, 1980), pp. 225–64; J. R. Lave and L. B. Lave, "Medical Care and Its Delivery: An Economic Appraisal," *Law and Contemporary Problems,* vol. 35 (1970), pp. 252–66.

17. John C. Goodman and Gerald L. Musgrave, *Patient Power* (Washington, D.C.: Cato Institute, 1992).

18. Gary M. Anderson, Dennis Halcoussis, Linda Johnston and Anton D. Lowenberg, "Regulatory Barriers to Entry in the Healthcare Industry: The Case of Alternative Medicine," *Quarterly Review of Economics and Finance,* vol. 40 (2000), p. 485.

19. Lave and Lave, op. cit.

20. Alex Kuczynski, "A Nip and Tuck with That Crown?," *New York Times,* May 16, 2004, p. 1.

21. Ronald S. Bond, John E. Kwoka, Jr., John J. Phelan and Ira Taylor Whitten, *Effects of Restrictions on Advertising and Commercial Practice in the Professions: The Case of Optometry* (Washington, D.C.: Federal Trade Commission, 1980).

22. Lee, Benham, "The Effect of Advertising on the Price of Eyeglasses," *Journal of Law and Economics,* vol. 15, no. 2 (1977), pp. 337–52.

23. State Auditor of Hawaii, *Sunset Evaluation of Barbering and Beauty Culture,* Report No. 01-02, January 2001.

24. Carroll and Gaston, op. cit.

25. Robert D. Atkinson and Thomas G. Wilhelm, *The Best States for E-Commerce* (Washington, D.C.: Progressive Policy Institute, 2002).

26. See Todd G. Buchholz, *Home Sweet Loan: How Secondary Mortgage*

Markets Changed America (Washington, D.C.: Homeownership Alliance, 2003), pp. 10–11.

27. David Autor, "Outsourcing at Will: Unjust Dismissal Doctrine and the Growth of Temporary Help Employment," National Bureau of Economic Research Working Paper W7557 (February 2000).

28. Marcello Estevao and Saul Lach, "The Evolution of the Demand for Temporary Help Supply Employment in the United States," National Bureau of Economic Research Working Paper 7427 (1999).

29. J. N. Dertouzos and L. A. Karoly, *Labor Market Responses to Employer Liability* (Santa Monica, CA: RAND Institute for Civil Justice, 1992).

30. Timothy J. Besley and Robin Burgess, "Can Labour Regulation Hinder Economic Performance? Evidence from India," Center for Economic and Policy Research Discussion Paper No. 3260 (March 2002).

SIX. Jobs v. Lawyers

1. Jeremy A. Leonard, "How Structural Costs Imposed on U.S. Manufacturers Harm Workers and Threaten Competitiveness" (Washington, D.C.: Manufacturing Institute for the National Association of Manufacturers, December 2003).

2. John Stossel, "Why America Needs Common-Sense Tort Reform," American Legislative Exchange Council Proceedings, 1994 National Orientation Conference.

3. Tillinghast-Towers Perrin, "U.S. Tort Costs: 2003 Update," February 2003; and Council of Economic Advisers, "Who Pays for Tort Liability Claims? An Economic Analysis of the U.S. Tort Liability System" (April 2002).

4. Ibid., p. 9.

5. Josh Gerstein, "11 States Seeking to Scupper Deal in Cosmetics Case," *New York Sun* (April 5, 2004). For more such cases, log on to over-lawyered.com, compiled by Walter Olson, author of several books on legal reform.

6. See Todd G. Buchholz, "Revolution, Reputation Effects, and Time Horizons," *Cato Journal* 8 (spring/summer 1988), pp. 185–97.

7. For Tobin's Q, see James Tobin, "Monetary Policies and the Economy: The Transmission Mechanism," *Southern Economic Journal* (April 1978).

8. Todd G. Buchholz and Robert W. Hahn, "Does a State's Legal Framework

Affect Its Economy?" U.S. Chamber of Commerce Institute for Legal Reform, AEI-Brookings Joint Center for Regulatory Studies (2003).

9. Emily Wagster Pettus, "Barbour: Legal Climate Hurt State in Push to Get Toyota Plant," Associated Press, April 26, 2004.

10. *Science,* December 15, 1989.

11. Joseph E. Stiglitz, Jonathan M. Orszag, and Peter R. Orszag, "The Impact of Asbestos Liability on Workers in Bankrupt Firms" (December 2002).

12. W. Kip Viscusi, "The Social Costs of Punitive Damages Against Corporations in Environmental and Safety Torts," *Georgetown Law Journal,* vol. 87, no. 2 (November 1998).

13. *American Bar Association Journal* (June 1997).

14. Daniel Kessler and Mark McClellan, "Do Doctors Practice Defensive Medicine?" *Quarterly Journal of Economics,* May 1996.

15. Peter Huber and Robert Litan, eds., *The Liability Maze* (Washington, D.C.: Brookings Institution, 1991) p. 7.

16. Tillinghast-Towers Perrin, "U.S. Tort Costs: 2000."

17. *Pelman* v. *McDonald's Corporation,* 2003 U.S. Dist. Lexis 707.

18. Sarah Ellison and Brian Steinberg, "To Eat, or Not to Eat," *Wall Street Journal,* June 20, 2003, p. B1.

19. "Better Clothes for Biggest Guys," *Wall Street Journal,* February 28, 2003, p. W14.

20. Todd G. Buchholz, "Burgers, Fries and Lawyers," *Policy Review,* No. 123 (February–March 2004), pp. 45–59.

21. Maggie Mulvihill, "At the Bar: Suits Target Ex-Employers for Defaming," *Boston Herald,* July 29, 2003.

SEVEN. Culture and Hollywood's Tin Ear

1. *Internet Movie Database News,* May 3, 2004.

2. Eugenia Baroncelli, Carsten Fink and Beata Smarzynska Javorcik, "The Global Distribution of Trademarks: Some Stylized Facts," World Bank Working Paper no. 3270, April 2004, p. 12.

3. Stephen Siwek, *Copyright Industries in the U.S.: 2002 Report* (Washington, D.C.: International Intellectual Property Alliance, 2002).

4. Glenn Lovell, "Movies and Manipulation," *Columbia Journalism Review,* (January/February 1993); Sharon Waxman, "Fade to Black," *American Journalism Review* (June 1997).

5. Suman Basuroy, Peter H. Boatwright and Wagner Kamakura, "Reviewing the Reviewers," Working Paper, April 2003.

6. Arthur De Vany and W. David Walls, "Bose-Einstein Dynamics and Adaptive Contracting in the Motion Picture Industry," *Economic Journal,* November 1996, pp. 1493–514. More recently, James Surowiecki, a financial writer for the *New Yorker,* has proclaimed *The Wisdom of Crowds* (New York: Doubleday, 2004).

7. Michael Medved, "That's Entertainment," *National Interest,* Summer 2002.

8. Arthur De Vany and W. David Walls, "Does Hollywood Make Too Many R-Rated Movies? Risk, Stochastic Dominance, and the Illusion of Expectation," *Journal of Business,* 2002.

9. Clint DeBoer, "Editorial: Ending Sex, Drugs & Violence in the Movies?" *Audioholics* (April 13, 2004).

10. See, for instance, S. Abraham Ravid, "Are They All Crazy or Just Risk Averse? Some Movie Puzzles and Possible Solutions," Working Paper, June 2002.

11. See S. Abraham Ravid, "Bambi as a Hedge," *Stern Business* magazine (Summer/Fall 1999), p. 19.

12. Kathy Chen and Leslie Chang, "China Takes Aim at Racy, Violent TV Shows," *Wall Street Journal,* May 24, 2004, p. B1.

13. Cris Prystay, "Creativity and Conservatism Compete in Ads for Asian Market," *Wall Street Journal,* May 10, 2004, p. A13B.

14. Seila J. Nayar, "Dreams, Dharma and Mrs. Doubtfire," *Journal of Popular Film and Television* (Summer 2003); Vikramdeep Johal, "Plagiarism as an Art Form," *Tribune of India* (November 8, 1998).

15. C. Samuel Craig, William H. Greene and Susan P. Douglas, "Culture Matters: A Hierarchical Linear Random Parameters Model for Predicting Success of U.S. Films in Foreign Markets," Stern School of Business, New York University (April 2003), p. 32.

16. Canadian Consulate General in Shanghai, *Do You Want a Big Mac or Rice? A Report on the Fast Food Industry in China* (Ottawa: Agriculture and Agri-Food Canada, April 2002).

17. Lech Walesa, "In Solidarity," *Wall Street Journal,* June 11, 2004, p. A8.

18. Christina Klein, "The Hollowing Out of Hollywood," Yale Global Online, Yale Center for the Study of Globalization (2004).

19. "U.S. Trade Representative 2004 'Special 301' Decisions on Intellectual Property," International Intellectual Property Alliance, May 3, 2004.

20. William P. Alford, *To Steal a Book Is an Elegant Offense: Intellectual Property Law in Chinese Civilization* (Stanford: Stanford University Press, 1997); Peter K. Yu, "The Second Coming of Intellectual Property Rights in China," Occasional Papers in Intellectual Property, no. 11, Benjamin N. Cardozo School of Law (2002), pp. 16–18.

EIGHT. Conclusion

1. Since the labor force would not actually grow by sixteen million, the benefits would show up as a combination of more jobs, better jobs and a higher standard living.
2. "Power in Your Hand," *Economist* survey, April 11, 2002.
3. See Mancur Olson, *The Rise and Decline of Nations* (New Haven, CT: Yale University Press, 1982) and Todd G. Buchholz, *New Ideas from Dead Economists,* pp. 247–63.